RUTH

GOD'S FAVOR WITH A CARESS OF TRUTH

I0167246

Robin) (Rochel) Arne

RUTH

GOD'S FAVOR WITH A CARESS OF TRUTH

*A*dvantage
BOOKS

A GENTILE PERSPECTIVE FROM THE RURAL SIDE OF LIFE

ROBIN (ROCHEL) ARNE

Ruth, God's Favor With a Caress of Truth by Robin (Rochel) Arne
Copyright © 2023 by Robin Arne
All Rights Reserved.
ISBN: 978-1-59755-767-2

Published by: ADVANTAGE BOOKS™
                  Orlando, FL
                  www.advbookstore.com

Scripture taken from the HOLY BIBLE, NEW INTERNATIONAL VERSION®. Copyright© 1973, 1978, 1984 by International Bible Society. Used by permission of Tyndale House Publishing. All rights reserved.

Library of Congress Catalog Number: 2023951774

First Printing: December 2023
23 24 25 26 27 28   10 9 8 7 6 5 4 3 2 1

Acknowledgements

God supports the work I do in all forms of goodness to my heart. I believe He is the one offering the knowledge and the hope of my progressive writing. This book is for the study of the market of the individual in search of light as to where home-front property is found. The lead of writing in the commission of the book of Ruth is a study in which man and land connect as a unity of growth and harmony. The light of the farming community is transparent to the eye when grain and fields are plentiful with a rich flavor of crops and creatures within the pastures. Many do not understand the hand of the Lord pierces the growing season along with the planting time. Harvest consumes the farmer as it is delicate in the manner of attention to bringing in the bread and butter with care from God. The retention of the bounty needs the appropriate drying mesh so discoloration and mold don't set in. Harvest features the love God holds to man in the way of being fed from the resource of the land and valley of light, where opportunity is gained by the refreshing of the spirit. The valley of dry bones spoken of in Ezekiel reflects on the progression of life toward growth in a new manner, meaning life eternal is a gateway from the Lord to His people. Call on the Savior and know Him in a personal way. He will grace your person, and you will gain an inheritance to the Most High, Father God.

Robin) (Rochel) Arne

FORWORD

The purpose of this study aid is…

This study will enhance the unity of God in each heart that invests in the knowledge of the Word of Ruth. The book of great knowledge is the Holy Bible. God offers us a connection to Him by way of the words He crafted for our support and gain. The Lord has gifted this writing to a community where many know the Savior as their own. I am one who serves the people with the intent to enlighten and support the authors in the field of development. Authors come in many forms. They can be laymen or type setters whose work reflects the design of growth in unity and support by way of commitment to subsidizing the internet with functioning material available for purchase and sharing. The field I serve in is related to the function ability of a concerned group who have invested in the local church and its relation to the surrounding boundaries. Our doors are open to the public for viewing, and this book is a result of a gift of insight to enhance knowledge about our way of life. Each verse I pursued was designed by the hand of the Father.

He gave the material of this unit of study. I placed today's way of living within the page content and applied its principles to our way of life. Look at Scripture for all your goal-making, but know people are a reflection of the spirit of God when they trust Him in a personal manner. The individuals this book manifested to serve is a broad witness. I hope to offer this course to many who come to our location for support in their walk with the Father. The gateway for this action is a united endeavor, and the offering God provides keeps our energy and stride pursuing the growth and building of our town and surrounding areas. The passage of hope I have placed within the circle of my sphere has been a plantation of moral gain. Many have come alongside my stand and delivered aid so the building could thrive.

Our community is knit in the bosom of the great I Am. We look to Him for support and inspiration, where we all serve Him with the intent of lifting Him up in praise.

God is located within our harvest of a witness, and He delivers many to our front doorway. We welcome many travelers along with the local talent of our community. No one is without an idea or a gift of knowledge, and we share our love for God with one another. Our actions trust the lead of God, and together, we tie as one in faith.

Just as the will of God is a unity of might, so is the stand of light all man offers to another for the sake of truth to be witnessed. Leading is made, and goals are developed as a body of gifted people. The way the lead is understood is an ever-present light from God above. Our goal is to plant and harvest the light God makes available to our spirit. By administering love to all, we shine in support and goal-making. God acknowledges us as a team, and we dine on this perspective. Carrying the load for a community should be partnered with the commission of strength the Father holds; this is how we blend as a community. The power of the great I Am is planted within our hearts, and we concede He is greater than we are. Our way of being supportive of His unity is to apply our gain to the outside world by sharing our Lord with all who come to our ground. Our flagpole of hope is the town square and the love we gain as we gather there. No gift is too great or too small when Christ is the focus of the giving. Our operation is a hope for the lost and a support platform for the weary or tired. Our plant of trust is so others may grow in faith and be carried to the cross for the bounty of a tight-knit unity where faith supports the heart and rewards flow as a gift of insight and a mature mental vision. Our ministry is for anyone needing more witness insight where love and faith abound. The level of commitment from God is visible in the ground maintenance and the structure of the garden of our hearts. We invest in care, so many may have a connection to the Most High when they visit our region of the nation. The load of the goal is not one person's outlook. Much investment has been given to detail for the presentation of strength you witness. The community builds as a group of willing hearts who pursue the will of the Father.

The love of God is forthright and the glue of our building desire. We capture His manner and feed the spirit He bestows within our hearts and minds. God operates with care, and His grace is our reward. Laboring for the truth is not a burden but a desire where we relate to God and His connection to our hearts. The planting of the church was a witness from generations of yesterday, and generations of today continue the unity. Growing a community takes an allegiance, and God is the operator of our support beam. Through His person, we desire to offer another the option of a tied heart to the great I Am.

Table of Contents

Robin) (Rochel) Arne

Unity Maker One

God's Caress Is A Support Beam

The lead of the Lord is genuine and supports man in his desire for growth in the love He holds.

The light of love from the Father was an entanglement of the heart, and man was weary from a long journey where family support was nonexistent. God had a plan for the family of Ruth to dissipate, and a new growth experience was to ensue. The timing of the Messiah was a focal point before the birth had taken form. God enacted the unity of the kinsman of Boaz to fall prey to the way of death, ensuring the future of the generations to the trust of Christ. God brought forward a bond for many to align in the manner of trust and guidance. The covering of the King would relate to the timing of grace offered by Jesus' death on Calvary. God built for man the faith and support of care when he delivered Naomi and Ruth to a new prosperity, which brought forth a new mental way of understanding the goal of family where hope can reside. The care of God was revealed when Naomi's husband passed and her sons as well. This opened the gateway for new beginnings. Naomi judged correctly and returned to the beloved home she had been swept away from. God pursued her with care when He aroused her instinct to adhere to the way of gaining prosperity according to the custom of the day. Naomi was a forthright individual. She brought hope to others by presenting a path in support of the great I Am. God has glory for man in the way of strength and support. He is a Waymaker in whom man is able to invest and build up another. The disposal of strength is not what brought Naomi to her homeland. It was the lead of God to her person.

Favoring her kinsman as a generational foster, Naomi pledged to offer the gift of hope to a man in the elder part of his stay as a recognized being in the community of the homeland Naomi supported. God never placed Naomi in an area she couldn't communicate with. Her desire to stand in unison as a caregiver and respected member of society was her choice. God knew Naomi was accustomed to the goal of building in favor of her clan. With the favor and support of God, Naomi found a relocated position available, and she sent Ruth to the field of a man she respected and trusted. God had a goal of bringing the light back into the heart of a woman who had been His child over time, and she pursued the Lord with care and uplifted guard, sponsoring in trust and hope. Naomi was a bride of the Lord, and she related to the good He represented in His Word.

God savers the will of man when it shines in favor and support of His person. God gifts man with integrity when the heart gains understanding. Man will digest the gain of God and be fed in the way of light and hope. The unity of God with His children is one of righteousness and support. God's leading makes a way where we are connected with Him in love. The hour of importance is always every minute of the day. Each vulnerable happening points to God, whether it be the unity of a child to his parent or the understudy of a person to his wife. All actions hold merit and value. Changing in unity does not enlighten the bond. It tears it down. The unity of God to His people is a glorious manner of standing. The light of the moon shines with integral beauty, but God is the revelation of care. The land in a field is bountiful, but God is the creator of all ground. Crops are abundant when rain is provided, and the sun incorporates with the earth. God is the crafter who made the unity of these transpire. God is always making grass sprout and sending rain to nourish the soil. He crafts and supports the unity of them all. If we perceive God as a righteous tool of strength, we connect with His person. When we portray God in the light and unite for the better of all, we adhere to His way of living. A community where many support man is a divested sponsorship of the heart. But a rural setting leaves the mind the unity where heart and earth are tied. Our ground in the rural setting supports the mouth and feeds the livestock. We ascertain the instruction of wise counsel, and crops are produced in a manner of strength. Fertilizer invests an element that gifts a plant more energy to grow and yield to the sun. Planting in the way of this is how we offer food of the heart to another. Our tithe is a fruit garden of love. Any being can incorporate the love God has into his lifestyle. Reading the Scriptures is what makes this avenue available. Little concern is ever placed in the way of possessions if the heart has been cared for by the truth of the great I Am. Looking at where the availability resides showers the heart with the knowledge God will adhere to the one who pursues a goal of gifted love in support of Him. Aligning the mind with the option of unity is not new to a people group who invest in the care God offers. Naomi understood this process. She planted in the grove of God the Father, knowing He would protect her spirit even when heartbreak had transpired within her spirit. Her husband was taken along with the financial guidance of her son. God is the real provider. In Him is favor, and genuine gifts of love always bloom.

Each settlement in the Midwest is a cover of unity provided by the will of the Father. The staked claim to property entailed man to group his belongings and travel across the country to gain an inheritance for growing an income in the way of seed and bounty of the animal element. All God provided established the land and made it thrive with a goal of strength in line with the knowledge God is righteous. Jesus is the way, the truth, and the life. His support connects our hearts and pours us a foundation of light, so man is able to adhere in strength and courage where the goal and light of unity is grafted to the heart. The resin of a cloud ensures the mind rain is about to spring on the plain. Our ladder of opportunity melts the desire of hope, and we express wealth in the manner of intent. The offering Naomi gave was for her daughter-in-law to know the Lord and King to come. She set the stage for Ruth to bind in the care she knew was real, and it centered her decision-making for the righteous Word of God to enter her heart and set in motion the bond of power. God offers man a connected manner of hope where the light of the Most High is present and uplifting. The soul of man is not what builds the bounty of a dream. It is the Lord thy God who makes a gateway and a unity in care where ideas flow, and good intent is a witness platform. The offering of unity is always at hand when the Savior is the one building. He will design the goal to align with the purpose of a glorified being, the great I Am. In the way God unites man to His person, there is gain and support. The helm of unity provided by the Lord is always right and true. God does not deal inwardly but with precise, goal-making grafts. The Lord is ever present, tying the heart to the dream. Many offerings will be under the layer of the build, so many will be able to withstand the time of trial when building is needed for an idea to have legs of strength. God is the supplier of the good intent, and in Him is the binding material of hope. With favor from Christ, land evolves into cities, and grocery lanes have a building site.

The offering of strength is good and plentiful when the Father has gifted the understanding to create for His namesake. The quest for unity is always a mainstay where the love of God is our common ground. When a person creates a garden, the heart of the earth is at the table during harvest time. The goal of the image of the bed for vegetables was the objective for the graft to stand. A table with wealth enables the body to be nourished, and the heart and mind attend to the good as well. Unity is the goal for the whole developed gift, so hands have to invest in weed removal as well as watering if dryness sets in. A horizon of hope is crafted at the first sign of growth. A sprout is an indicator God is prospering in the union of the garden. When a crop duster sprayers the layer of dust upon the heart of a field, he is paving the earth with a guard where bugs cannot infest and swarm the produce. This protection is a guarantee the crop will be supported in care. Just as this action atones the manicure of farming, God is ever doing the same for our care and support. With the favor of Christ, our heart is protected by the blood of the Lamb. The layer of blood poured onto our spirit is a calculated bounty of love and secure growth. We adhere to the medium. God favors our spirit with His, and understanding of His person ensues. The cause and effect of the pilot's skill level when dusting is done is not of the average person. Much skill has been acquired, and time in the cockpit has made recognition of the controls so the pilot can fly with comfort and control. The reward is a job well done, and the benefit of an income plays a role that supports the continued opportunity of more invested positions of standing. The community where a crop duster resides needs to correlate with the control of the environment in need of his skill level.

Today, many observe the way a plane travels but have no knowledge of the operation of farming beneath the wings. Today, there is a respite where favor is gifted through the internet and the volume of television material to watch. But farm management of today is not like it used to be. Most farms and ranches cover many acres, and they support much labor. Farm equipment does the work of many men. The tractor used in today's farming community towers above the man who drives it down the road. Just as Boaz farmed in his stand, man today has the convivence of technical support. Boaz was not enabled in this manner. He had a crew of men who harvested his grain, but the same God who made the wheat in Boaz's field made the grain that produced the bread you served on your table a time or two. Every individual who eats flour has been supported by the farmer God blessed. A light had been grafted, and the understanding had risen within the mind so expertise could ensue and not be lost through doubt. God delivers to all mankind the understanding to pursue a goal of length where employment is acquired to maintain a family or the individual himself. God lights the path for progress, and hope is a gift for the heart.

Today is not a hindering sight as man has the forward plan to pursue his directive and lean into the Father. All the goals of man are made reality when the Father lifts the heart and mind into a forward path of light and gives the desire to prosper as a whole. Most people pursue a plan and build wealth step by step. God is the coverage where the heart supports the demand, and fruit garners the way ahead. God delivers a planting of strength, and the goal comes to light in a manner of unity by which God is revealed as the source of the gain. If a person feels disconnected from God, looking toward Him with good intent will adhere his spirit to the bounty of knowing Him. An invested person aligns his time and pursues God with favor. This is where unity is found. Leaning into the light is what proves worthy to our spirit, and the bind of love will scope the forward intent, and love will blossom within. Reading the Scripture of Ruth leads the mind into the instruction God has a purpose for the generations of all man. Each person in the verses of the Book reflects the love God had for them. Even Ruth recognized the unique way God offered her Naomi with her wise counsel and her support of love to her as a daughter. Whether the goal is to guide someone into the knowledge of the love God has or to plant the truth of salvation, all of Scripture supports God as a whole being of good intent. God's light is kind and supportive. He makes paths that guide and lead in care. By His person, man learns and crafts in the light of a true, integral personality. His manner is righteous and good.

All of God is light, so we need to think of Him as our personal, guidance counselor, where truth will always lead with good intent. The vocal pattern of strength He portrays is always rich and flavorful, with good instincts and righteous manners.

God aligns our will with His way of being. When light grafts to our hearts, we learn and develop a path with strength and trust. Leaders are bound in the care they offer. A tyrant never holds the heart of the people he rules over. He is an issue of disgrace in the heart of the faithful. Even in the case of lost unity, God is the King of righteousness. Our Savior is ever righteous and good. Boaz understood that man was weak when he spoke of the transaction for gaining more revenue. The plan of the younger kinsman was for the property to pass over into the estate of Ruth, where his name would not flourish, but hers would. This is not what his desire manifested as. He preferred to inherit more of a reward, so he released the value to another. Often, we miss the sound gift God presents us with when we seek too much wealth in the place of good pursuits. Not all wealth is a positive when it only adheres to our bank account. There can be wealth in the form of a bond with someone who respects your person over that of one who feeds your account but represents you in a negative manner.

A league of nations can build many roads and avenues, but not all lead to a tower of opportunity where gold is discovered and care is made available. When operating in unity with a prosperous intent, we must determine the motive and where our hearts reside. Favor is not subjective when God is the person you claim to stand guard with. The love of the King is a signing where strength and guidance are tied in unison, and hope is on the horizon for the period of the invested outcome. A future of intent is what sets our hearts in motion. Building to acquire only net worth will lead to losses and misgivings.

Doubt is a sure message of loss, and it can be digested as an avenue where the lead is not of Christ in that God never allows the heart the option of failure. When God is the lead in our building, glory arrives within, and it is recognized as belonging to the great I Am. When we dine on the unity God offers our hearts, we embrace His good care. We develop with sporting wisdom, and unity is our desire. The gain from God is ever beneficial, and we recognize good intent. Our lead becomes that of a personal stand, and light is our caregiver. God is the Waymaker and the guardian of the heart. So, practice good stewardship as if owning a piece of property that contains Christ Himself, which is what your heart really is. You are an abbreviation of Christ in that you represent Him in faith when you profess that He is with you as your Lord and Savior. Remember, all righteous acts secure the heart and lead it to an assembly of righteous good.

The unity of Christ to man is a gain for unity where the reproof is not of man. Meaning God is the light and the source of integral strength. God has fathered the man of His unity by giving light to many who pursue Him in faith. The support God offers is a gift and light where all find favor. The support of God is a unity in tides of change with visual grafting, which adheres to the call of His namesake, Jesus Christ. Pursuing God is a mainframe way of being. The power of the Lord is steadfast and supportive, with hope at its side in the manner of strength and gifted love. All the worship of the King is a gain for man, and his heart will grow in truth. The light the King guides us in creates a goal of undying faithful hope. The bond of God to man is a unity that never loses the framework of delight. God's power is unified within our minds and clear hope springs forward where many ideas gain traction. Allowing the favor of the Most High a pathway within our heart is a decided manner of good favor. It breeds in care, and a united platform of strength guides our hopes and dreams to become a reality. God has gifted the plowman a road of earnings, which is an example of workmanship and perseverance. God is tied to our mind when we read and apply His bind of love from the Word He grafted us to learn from. He exudes the length and fullness of great intent by operating in our best interest. The farmer has a gift of maintaining the ground and delivering goals of crops and livestock where many are supplied support and nutrition compliments the formation.

How God manages the goals of all people is representative of how vast His abilities reach across the scope of all things great and small. Leaning on the truth, the mighty God of all favors man above any other living creature supports the knowledge God holds us in His image and sets us on the scale of importance. The label we hold is that of a child. To God, we are His children, the bride He holds close and breathes hope and guidance into. All of our character relates to the mirror image when we act in accordance with the great I Am. The goal of building in favor of growth for the benefit of another is the farmer's way. The seed offering comes by way of the salesman, but the growth is when the farmer has planted the grain of seed, and God is the one to make it flourish and thrive. The statement of faith the farmer possessed was one of character designed by God's hand. The salesman who placed the seed order had the insight to offer hope that God would bring the seed to a viable, gifted growth. Man has doctored the seed to make it more stable, but God is the one who gives him the knowledge of how to aid this germination technique.

God supports man as a whole, and by His person, man learns to obtain a rich understanding God loves him as His child. A flower in the yard is a manner of strength in the designer's heart before it is recognized as a reality. Many gardens prosper by having fruits and vegetables they can partake of because of hard work and the bounty of knowledge God bred into their being. Whether a man is extensive in his knowledge or slight in understanding, God is still the Waymaker who provided the mental gain. God harbors the heart and calculates the gear units that supply man with courage and desire, so bounty builds. The offering of God's will to our hearts comes by way of a whisper from His person. The light God crafts is personable and manicured in the way it presents in unity. God favors anyone who aligns with good intent for those who offer the range of their spirit. The connected bond is a gift where light is abundant and holy, made by the Father of all mankind. A unity is not a slight contrast but a replica of God's power to another within the person aligning in care and support. If you desire a unity gift, trust the Lord to design a way for it to build and grow. God makes man His light in the way of talent and hope. When a body of faith operates as one, much gain presents the scene of entanglement as a light of guidance and clear opportunity.

If a cattle operation is on the plain of life for the farmer, much knowledge must be adhered to. The management is laid barren when no one has the gift of knowledge in treating ailments or the feeding and setting in alignment with pasture time. Rotations bring flourishment to the ground of grass where the cattle feed and bear calves. The ground produces a home and a guardian way of maintaining unity with the support of livestock to man. Everyone either attempts to or is gifted with growing a living being. Whether it be a fish or a cow, it takes knowledge to keep them in the way of growth and support of livelihood. The decision to farm brings many ties to a region.

Man needs one another for much in the way of support. Machinery costs have risen to that of some homes and far beyond those numbers for much of what is required to operate in the correct manner of intent, which will enable a farm to succeed. Glowing reviews do not tabulate as income. There must reside good manners of growth in the way of production versus the fuel and maintenance fees. This operation sustains itself due to the man and his relationship goals with the God of all. In conjunction with others, many farms bind the loss and expenditures as a body. The lifestyle is conducive to a full-time job with no vacations or days off. A farm community has much in the way of wealth as the people act with care for one another. Just as Ruth was blessed by the witness Naomi offered to her, man in the farming community gains recognition as a worker of light when he applies with grace the hope of future unity. The tally of the bill for a goal of great importance is what many ascribe to it. The outstanding numbers before tax restrictions do not reflect the real bond of patronage applied. A farm has several expenditures, all of which require the bank to regulate and gift. Farming holds a value only upon the sale date of the assets. However, man has a gift in the way of management, so he can withstand the expenditures and operate with care and support while building an equitable homestead.

To grow and maintain a bounty such as Boaz had acquired was a skilled representation of the workers and the people in the boundary of the land he held. Boaz was articulate in the understanding of how property changing hands was pursued and leveraged. Ruth held promise to Boaz, where the kinsman closest to her found her title, not to his style of managed gain. Boaz pursued the goal of lifting up another and allowing the growth to better his stake with God. His actions supported the life and goodness of care for Ruth and her mother-in-law. Naomi was a woman who believed in the righteous way Boaz would operate toward her personally. She knew the God she had bound her life toward was good and merciful. Just as Christ is to us, so was the unity between God the Father and Naomi. Jesus and the Father are one, but Christ had not presented Himself to the people in full view until after His death and resurrection. But we know He was viable before time began in our accord of understanding. God has a goal for all mankind, and He desires for man to connect with Him in a stand of light and care. We assume our heart's desire is our own gifted thought process. When in actual acknowledgment, it is a perimeter God has built within us. Dreams build and absorb our minds in the manner of built-up intentions if we proceed with them in a standard of trust. God is the one to make a gateway and to relieve our burden so we can maintain the connected graft of His person to our being in a developed stage of guidance. If we favor the Lord, many inventive, opportune dreams can be realized. God adheres to our hearts, and in doing so, we invest in the love He offers, and we visualize opportunity as a whole.

God's alignment is a gift and a support beam where our hearts and minds build in unison. Just as God moved Ruth because of Naomi, we are led by the favor God bestows towards us. If you feel a nudge to grow in a new location, God may deliver you growth in a new manner. Ruth was guided through the care of a mother who did not claim her as her birth daughter, but she did love her as her own. Many times, we fall into line with a family that isn't by blood or inheritance. Friends lead our goals, and in some cases, we tie directly to the goal they put forth. God binds in the way of intent and hope. With Him as our lead, we build in a bountiful way. The unit of one is limited in the power it holds, whether it be a machine operator or a farmer with a small building site who gardens for a living. We all need support at some point, and looking to God to deliver a unit of support proves a goal of good form. Our adherence to God is what sets our lives on the track of upright living. Favor in the manner of built homesteads is developed with many hands. A lineage of strength is one of care and a unified outlook. The person of God carries our dreams and builds them in the hearts of others so relational goals align and gifted hope unfolds. God's perfect line of respect shows us who He is as a right and true leader of the heart. Naomi was gifted the desire to return to her family for protection as her unity of ties was derailed. The death of her son procured for her the need to retain her heritage and align with the will of the Father. God entertains our hearts with a goal and a dream where hope flourishes and unity is witnessed. Our drive is one of protected unity when the power of the Lord is our caretaker. God is a being of unity. He favors when we operate in unison with those around us. The relationship we hold with the populous around our area of livelihood is barren without the goal of building as a group. Staking a manner of life-giving hope supports the need and leads the health to thrive where man and God are tied with support. The lead of God is ever available, just as it was with Naomi and Ruth. Our leaning into the man of Jesus shows favor is the tie we adhere to. God did not desire for man to be alone. He grafted him a wife to seal his heart with support and love for another, where both came together as one. The desire of man to build is retrospect of the unity God placed in Adam when only creatures roamed the Garden of Eden. Man desires a reflective gift to communicate with. That is where we find the drive and ambition to relish livelihood.

Robin) (Rochel) Arne

Unity Maker Two

God Factors All Things

Guidance is light when God is the gift tying the perception of strength.

Grafting to the manner of intent is what determines the goal set forth. Just as Naomi supported Boaz by offering Ruth toward his person, there was a dream breeding and building for a people group to align and fall into the goal of inheritance for the Son of man to rise and claim the gateway for all to know Him as Lord. The power of God to man is not seen by anyone who does not look to Jesus as their Lord. Only faith-believing individuals can relate to the manifest way of light God shelters man with. Unifying our goal of favor toward that of Jesus gifts the heart the care and drive it needs to operate in the way of justified hope. God delivers the goal and fills the heart with care and support so as to enlighten those in the path with a dream to fulfill His will. All the ways of many does not mean success will abound. God must desire the outcome to breed as light where He is glorified and given praise. Working for the good of unity is a gift of knowledge that strikes the bond of strength of an appetite of Christ to be made a realization. Ruth did not claim Christ, nor did she portray the unity Naomi had, but she made the choice to follow the example of Naomi and learn and grow in the way of truth. Who we follow sets the way for others to see and comprehend our Father is good and righteous. Look at where Naomi took her standard of life. When she lived apart from her residence of trust known to her as home, she suffered a loss and then returned for support from family and unity members of her like-minded way of being. The gift of light it offered was favor from on high. God never forgets His children, nor does He remove His hand of covering when they change location or reef of standard.

The alignment of care God gifted the people Naomi was tied to gained in the way of hope. Both daughters-in-law did not follow the God of Naomi. One separated and returned to the false impression and did not prosper in the way of unity gifted to Ruth. Ruth became the mother of the Most High by lineage in the grandmother portrayal. It was generations away, but the path was laid forth, and the King was granted a birthhood of good favor. God supported the unity of Himself to His people when Jesus was declared

Savior to mankind. The lighting of care was not a candle in the wind. It was a mainstay that never lost footing or ground cover. All of man benefited and thrived as a whole when the Savior manifested as man in a veil of strength where hearts could receive Him in truth and support.

God's alignment in favor was a connection to the heart of man where support was garnered and fed a live vessel of strength. The timetable was not visible to many, but those who followed the Word of the Lord understood the arrival when the star lit up the heavens. Shepherds were tending their flocks, and people were gathering one to another to adhere in unity over the wonderment and awe of the King Jesus. A baby tied man to God in a manner no other would ever be able to administer. All of mankind gained a faith and support player of great measure. The timing of Christ's birth was a plain way for God to bestow His righteous love to many. A guidance unity was not the only benefit to man. The death and resurrection of Jesus is what built the tomb of death into a gateway of light where man could tie himself to God in a personal form. Many gain unity today because God favored them with the knowledge Jesus is the path of light. Our bond of light comes forth when we stand in unison with Christ and show many the lighted path we ourselves adhere to. The long-awaited King now resides with the Father, and they are tied forever as one in faith and kind entitlement. God is made of truth and goodwill. In Him is the avenue of gain many desire for their own personal, manifested manner of growth. Knowing the Savior is not difficult to obtain. Trust Him to honor your intent with the guidance of His care, and you will be made in His image. You will gain in the way of hope, and faith will be a daily investment toward the love you hold for God.

God creates in care and unity when a person subjects his heart toward the love of Jesus. He is the gateway to God the Father. Naomi knew the Father, and she raised her children to do the same. How we understand this is due to the unity she offered her daughter-in-law, Ruth. Ruth learned by the example Naomi presented her in the manner of gratefulness of her support. The lead Naomi offered was one of unity. She tied her stand with that of Ruth, who had lost her lifestyle in the same manner she had. The two walked in a partnership to maintain the unity they knew in one another's care package of grace. The time before them was a trial, but the loving hand of the Father was seen each step of the way.

God is faithful and supports man when a unity of hope is crafted in the heart. A solid investment is a gain when the available holdings reflect the light of the King. The manner of a gift to share holds the plan and will of the Father where ideas flow, and understanding binds to the care package. A commitment of life is viable, and growth can be adhered to by standing in faith with the Lord. The unity of Christ to His people is one of total elation where the mind grafts the knowledge put toward the King. Alone, man gains by way of invested labor, but with Jesus, a bounty lights the heart and mind and soon favor compiles, and the gift of light shines for many to see. If you underline the good intent and find labor is what comes to the table, you have a guardian manner of insight. There may align others who desire the goal of the union, and a plan will emerge in favor of supporting the Lord and His will. When reading the book of Ruth, take note of the manner in which justice was made visible in the workroom of the man Boaz. He was righteous and secure in the manner he destined his guidance toward. He did not come out and attack Ruth for her staying at his feet and placing her body at the foot of his bed. The threshing floor was not a rest bed but a holding room for workers and men of invested wealth in the way of grain and tares. The separation of the two was done by hand, which brought dust and dirt inside the barrier of restraint. God permitted favor when the gateway of strength for the women from a distant land came to find shelter in the wake of someone within their circle of kinsmen.

Naomi supported the goal of building a plan that enabled the two women to find shelter and a lifestyle of good form. Ruth gained a man in her life who protected her with his stand of importance. The land supported the family of unity, and both the woman Naomi and the man Boaz had an idea of unity between the two. God showed his map for going forward to their hearts, and much building in net worth aspired within. The lineage of man to God was the goal of Christ and His Father, the great I Am.

Look to the north when you think about cold weather and determine where the line of warmth begins and where the division resides. God made a center where light shines and adheres to the heart of the farmer. The Midwest is a bountiful home front, and solid witnessing builds the heart and offers it freedom in growth and the company of light. The people of the community in the breadbasket of America are equipped with the ability to maintain a property when the weather is in the freezing stage, along with the heat of summer where the temperature can reach 100 degrees. This builds the body a shield of goal making so there are various, aligned qualities of goods to protect against the elements. People gain an understanding of how to shelter the grain and support it in extreme weather conditions. Monitors and devices of hope are placed within the property of a farm, so spoilage does not invest in the goods man has harvested from the field. The supplement of hope from God is wisdom. God is the provider of the gift of fruit where money and invested time meet as one. The light of God shines and festers a love of standing that portrays unity and care. God never leaves an idea to rot with no foundation.

Look at how God served the women of the era in the day of Ruth when he offered shelter to their facility, known as the common ground for slaves and widows to glean the leftover produce that had fallen to the floor of the field. Today, we have Combines the size of a small home, and much of the loss no longer exists. The machine itself takes liberty with the head of the wheat stalk and retrieves the golden harvest a kernel at a time. The management to maintain the rod of strength is an expense of great, major pocket booking. Many find this job rewarding as it is a time when man is able to reside in the comfort of an interior structure without the dust of the day building up within his person. Years past, like in the Ruth and Naomi era, this comfort did not exist. They had to glean the crop and beat it with boards or sheaths of whips splitting the grain from the stalk. The wheat stubble was used to make straw bricks of clay and dirt, then baked to remove impurities, thus producing a bond of strong witness material. Many find this a way of making unique structures of artwork. The burning of the straw sets in motion a smoke where elements adhere to the outer ridge of the body of art, causing it to smoke a pattern where burned images are placed by the Father's hand. Burning clay is done in a manner of delicate formation so the artwork does not receive breakage in the burning. Pottery is an image of God, as man is not the one to create the magic that transpires within the kiln firing.

God builds in unity with the goal of man, and He maintains the desires of structure, so growth is a process enjoyed by the heart. Jesus crafted with his hands as a carpenter, which relates to the heart of a man who designs in wood and sculpture making. A present-day identity for this is the tower in Paris, where poorly constructed material erected an applique of doubt. The intent was to create a unique landmark of faith, but in its place stands a barrier of doubt, representing a loss to the build. God makes and designs with light, so a true bond is made visible. A carpenter who builds with Christ makes gifts of talent, and hope is grafted. Christ built the bridge for man to align in good faith with His person for all eternity. God enabled the union per the cross and the bloodshed that was poured upon sin as a whole. God is the gift we all need to claim for a life of good favor, and light. The unity of God to man is made viable when feeding the spirit with the Word of truth in our unity to Him.

God gifts man with the desire to perform out of his element on many occasions. If a goal is within your heart, but there is no path to follow, lean into the hand of the King and look at where He has placed your dream. Are you recording the goal and stating it as a righteous way ahead? Are you acting with a pure intent so many may find support from God? Do you see others building with your goal, or do you stand in a simple bond of grey desire with no other standing in your circle of faith? God can operate as one with an individual, but pursuing a dream with many builds a character and a support group that affixes the heart in favor of God. A token faith does not support the love God holds toward your heart. Look at how Naomi stood in care for Ruth and how she claimed the goal of a family with her as her blood inheritance even though Ruth was not of the same lineage. Naomi partnered with Ruth and brought favor to them both. God lights the hearts of those who are tied to many, where a dream and a gift of strength can be aligned with truth to create a statement of favor from on high. Christ is at the helm when man builds to work with others in a supportive manner. A table is not set for just one person at a Thanksgiving banquet. So, plant your dream with the goal of finding the strength and unity of Christ, and His favor will build you an open pathway to gain in the manner of the intent He desires. The light of the King is a bond and sacrament that speaks to the message of the cross. Favor is the will of God, so build with the support of truth as the headway and unity to design by. God will show the manner of His goal, and you will adhere to His instruction with free will and drive. God is the one who desires the unity of man to Himself, so building in the way of support to another is what gains us favor. Look to God to better intend support, and your heart will dine on unity. This unity will be made steadfast, and the gravitational pull from God to you will align with support, and a forward trial will ensue, meaning light will be gifted to you, and you will know how to proceed in care and guidance for others to learn by your witness.

God is the support beam that aligns the will of Himself to another who believes in His person. Grafting to the light God supplies gives the heart a path and a guidance hope of support. Unity was the drive that presented from Ruth to her mother-in-law Naomi. The tie that enabled them to remain as mother and daughter was a gift in the manner of unity with a representation of faith. Naomi was the lead and support plant who favored God and taught His way of life to another. Through the support, this offered the goal and bond of growth, so the two women found a walk of faith, which led them to Christ and the goal of salvation. How this transpired was in the name of God the Father. The people who gained the inheritance of unity with Christ before His birth realized God was the person of the great I Am. They recognized God was the gift of support where man could obtain favor from the Lord. Sacrifices were the trade of a witness in the day of Naomi and Ruth. Their sins were covered by the sacrificial lamb of a creature, not Jesus, but the symbolic form He represented. A sacrifice today is not needed as Jesus paid the fee for all to receive eternal life by way of faith in His person. A unity must be present in order for there to be a relationship. This is the goal of God for man. This is what sets the layer of truth within man and God as one. The one who operates the unity is God the Father. It is by His goal of life eternal that we receive salvation by the blood of Jesus, who died for our gain. Our sins are washed clean because of the death of Christ on Calvary. The unity of the Father became flesh and bone by the manner of Christ's birth, death, and resurrection. The tide of strength is that of a union where God supports the bond of strength man has to Him. The care of God in our favor is the gift of salvation. Grace is the measure used when God applies the unity. Ourselves, we are not able to stake a guidance to eternal life with God. He must be the one to align our heart and draw it to His person. We have free will, so the option to reject the offering is made available. However, life apart from God is dark, and no adherence is made available upon death. Accepting Christ before the marker of death strikes is the stand of life. Man has no understanding of the day or the hour of his passing. This is where trust must enter the heart. The favor has to be bought and claimed before the unity of time ends, where life has gone into the state of eternal time. There are no second chances once the last breath has been consumed. Release the guard of doubt and make Jesus the one you cleave to. Naomi understood God the Father was the Waymaker for her personal quest of life purpose.

God pursues man for a righteous manner of good, moral enlightenment. By the power of Christ, man is shown the way to present as a whole. God crafts the skill, and He is the way to build better and forthright goals. The support of God will align when all factors are adhered to. In the event your heart displays a bond for others to learn from, wait, and let God be the one who guides the team He is putting forth. Give Him the loan and let Him be the one to deposit the material to craft the embodiment of purpose you dream of. Take the helm when the door opens, and there is clear representation being expressed. God has a call to that of Himself to all who claim Him as their personal Savior. The intent of Christ was to be an alignment that supported man to the way of unity the Father held. The straw of Naomi's day was not gleaned and purified as it is today. Our witness of growth is visible as man no longer has to tie himself to the back of a mule to gain more stretch of ground as a complete field to operate and control. Our unity in God is factored in when the knowledge He has set forward is that of clear goal-making. Find your purpose and support those who desire to act in accordance with the Lord. You will find a bond where strength and love support one another. Operating with the instruction of caregiving is what determines whether the Lord is with the plan or whether it is man's desire alone without His counsel. Stand as a caregiver and align with Jesus. Truth will ride on the heart, and a love for many will craft to you. You will recognize God and see

His person in the build where others are entangled and led to the same ownership you are invested with. The perfect commission of light will be seen, and others will attribute the dream to that of the Most High.

Plan building is a goal, but it needs the desire of man to be accomplished. Look at Naomi as a witness who knew God and His objective for her life. God implements the unity, and a bargain of knowledge flows forth. The detail of man to God is a supplement of hope and an advancement of guidance where man unites in the way of light to the heart. Favor is bestowed when man dines on the instruction of the Most High. Support is understood by the one who favors the light of God.

Building in structure is a gift in the way it adheres to the heart and staples the love to itself. God is the deal of unity that brings favor and a heightened love for mankind. All the wisdom Solomon had made for a cast of unity where God was seen as the goal intent and the barrier of infringement was not made visible. Meaning the Savior had not yet been revealed. The great God of all mankind is always in the stay of favor when a person believes the Lord is who He claims to be. Support is seen when man dines on the instruction supplied by God's hand. In the event man forgets who God is to him, favor is removed, and losses ensue. The plan of unity from God to man is one of solid invested time and support. When we apply our love and desire to that of God, our understanding of Him grows and builds with trust. God supports our lifestyle when the bounty of the heart reflects Him in a righteous manner. God's love is solid and a strength of great magnitude where all He does is a desired gain of unity. Our own reflective manner is not forthright when God is not the reason we build. God gifts us with the glue where man to God is a staple of good design that projects an element of greatness. The build of strength comes forward where it is called into action. This can be a witness to our testimony, and support is seen as a whole in the party of others who claim Christ for themselves. Building is a comparative manner that holds many captive in the light of hope. A town's witness is expressed when people gather with the goal of declaring Christ is Lord over their homes and fields of growth. A business will administer a light if it balances the unity of God to its magistrate of goods and services. The title of man to God comes by way of Christ on the cross of life. When God put forth the bond of His goal, man understood the claim as righteous, where man is tied to God in a personal manner. Naomi understood God was real, and she set a standard for her daughter to gain this union. She witnessed the goal of the stated union and shared the knowledge of God to her person. Naomi was righteous, and she held fast to the understudy God was who He claimed to be. The goal of Christ through her person was one lineage. The Son of God was to follow the bloodline of Boaz and Ruth, and He was to reside in their heritage for eternal recognition. Man has known favor as a result, and by their commitment one to another, a birth of righteous intent was brought to life. The Caretaker of mankind is the great I Am, and He is the one who grafted the light through His Son. God designed the birth and the death to be a unity of great magnitude where all of mankind could obtain a unity with His person. None are forgotten or left behind when they believe in the Lord Jesus Christ as their personal Savior. God is the way for man to adhere to the real unity He grafted since the beginning of time. God had a plan and a goal that enabled the life of all people to remain steadfast and supported with unity between Himself and the partner of all.

God ties to man, and He develops the bond of strength where man to Himself is enlightened and fed in truth. God supports all of mankind. He does not play favorites, nor does He acknowledge only the gifted. Who He cleaves to is the one who casts his heart toward the graft God put forth in the way of Jesus to the recognized heart of good intent. The goal of the gift was the way it presented to all of mankind, not just an elect few. The support of unity the Father holds is made complete by the blood of Jesus. The example of unity displayed on Calvary was a sight of pure, honest support where teaching of the care from God to humans was understood. The black of the day when death had its time was small in comparison to the bond reflected by the person of Jesus. Death was an integral part of the testimony of God and how He loves His child along with the people of the earth. For all time, God has operated with support for the one who chooses Him as His standard and believes He is the Waymaker.

United in the connection is the gift of knowledge that speaks to the grace of God and how He alone is the great I Am. None can compare to how He operates or protects man. Think about the manner of Boaz to Ruth. He led her to his field for protected care and support from his crew of laborers, where she was able to provide for Naomi and herself with enough grain to last more than was required for the term of a week. How we stand with this gift of enlightenment is the term they shared in the care of his intent, and they were fed with hope over the course of days, which leads one to the understanding the time had come for more developed unity from God to Ruth. This example proved the claim God was with them. Naomi had a just influence, and by her support, Ruth was given the bond of strength required to learn of God's care in the manner of wheat and grain supplied for strength of the body. Ruth did not suffer from hunger, nor did she lose in the way of protection as God provided her with the coverage of Boaz's people to her steadfast harvesting of the field reported on paper as that of the farmer in support of her walk with integrity toward him alone and not that of a younger man. God drew Ruth toward the tying of an invested bond with the Caretaker of righteousness. Boaz was a man of character who reflected a strength of support toward the women God drew home to be with others who invested in Him on a whole of unity where desire met with strength.

God directs the heart, and He makes a way for strength to be gifted in a care unit of integral support. If you are indisposed and have no guidance as to how to proceed, look at the way God designed Ruth and Naomi to follow His lead. God led the spirit of good intent into Naomi, and she, in turn, supported the work God had on the table of understanding. Naomi stood in a righteous manner, not yielding to the temptation of other gods to pursue. Naomi had the influence of the Most High, and as a result, strength was garnered, hope bled forth where faith was built upon, and recognition of unity was bestowed in the manner of a marriage of tied dreams. Boaz had not known a woman as his wife, and old age had crept upon him, but because Naomi recognized him as a kinsman of character, life became a drive of unity where a man was granted a reprieve through the lineage of the Savior.

The ties of the spirit operate in unity with the King, and we are led with knowledge of how to invest with insight. Building for the better of a community has merit, and in the reflection of Christ, great hope is made viable. A plan of length can bring to the table a place where many prosper. Building for the sake of Christ brings a gain of recognition that cannot be denied. If you favor a support measure and have a desire for an opportune way of gifted strength, look at how Naomi invested in the relationship she knew as a family in a region that supported God. She divulged how to possess favor by supplying the knowledge of pursuing God as an example to live by. God offered her strength, and she, in turn, revealed to Ruth how to know the great I Am. When a goal of bonding ensued, God released the love he held, and growth became intertwined in the heart of Ruth. As a result, she, in turn, yielded to the will of the Father, and growth was given wings where the heart and the mind united in the support of the God she had been instructed to know. Allowing the favor of God to build and bond in the manner He has injected into a people group is where unity is transposed to a body of faith, and support is the outcome for all. Leading in the way of decision-making is a path for the clear of mind, not the lost or dejected. If you favor growth, look to wise counsel, and leadership will abound. God operates where He is welcome, so make Him the leader of all your goal-making. In Him is the light and guidance of the great I Am. The gift of unity is a clear hope from God to man where the heart transcribes to the Father and His path of enlightenment. In the offering of light, there is a unity of inspiration and guidance, so man is able to build and have hope. With God at the helm of the unity, gifted knowledge always unfolds in a pattern of formidable grafting. This is a unity all its own in the way it adheres to the mind when an idea is made visible. Desiring a build is God at work within the light of His person. God performs righteous maneuvers, and by His mental stability, man is given clarity. The offering of God to His child is far superior in the acknowledgment that a righteous, integral build is taking form. When God builds in the heart of man, He manifests light, and good intent is viable. When Naomi desired to return to her homeland, the faith she contained within was a support platform that God would lead her to safety. She stayed the course and fed on the truth that God was a caregiver. The support she needed was met, and Ruth was made her guardian in the way of marriage to Christ's heritage line, with Boaz as the leader and guide representative. Boaz supplied the needs, and both women were protected and cared for.

The supplier of the good intent was both parties, so unity was made a clean representation of the Most High. Both had a purity in that none sought to cause or inflict a loss to the person of the other. Naomi directed Ruth in how to perfume herself to present as a clean representative in line for the kinsman to accept her as his wife on the stand that she and he would marry. God organized the acceptance of Boaz to Ruth even though he was older than she was. Age was not significant in the day of tying one clan to another, yet from a woman's perspective, it would be of concern. Boaz was a man of integrity in the way he presented security to Ruth when she required a coverage of protective guardianship in the field where other men harvested on behalf of the master who owned the field. The care and support were gifts Ruth understood, and it bonded her to the Christ element of faith. The Lord was at work grafting to the Father His intent, and the two operated as one on behalf of the people in the territory of lineage Christ was to rein within. How this was made opportune and how it came to be could only be mastered by God Himself. The Father of all mankind knew what needed to happen, and He made a way for truth to be distributed to the hearts and minds of both women as they invested in the manner of faith toward the person of God. Both Naomi and Ruth supported the Lord, and both, subsequent one to another, found favor and truth because God orchestrated the love He held in support of their path in life, where unity blended and the call from God was made plain.

Divine unity is a gift where man to God is a mainstay within the love God holds for all people. The light of truth is a quest many miss and lose as a result of rejecting the light God offered freely by way of the ministry He developed through the blood of Christ on Calvary. God is a path of bright hope, and by His guidance, we see clearly how to work and serve one another. In retrospect, we underline the good in our lives and forget the days of loss because hope resides in our spirit. The bulk of hope is due to God operating within our person. He manifests and supports our desires when they align with good intent and support the goal of binding man to the person of Jesus. Our own desire to control the outcome of any design element is made viable only when we lean into God and let Him lead.

God the Father is a caregiver in whom love and honor abide. In Him is the resolute knowledge that He is the planner and developer of all things righteous with good intent. God Almighty is careful in His style of gain. He develops men to perform for His way of being, and He acknowledges their hopes and goals. When light is the focal point, unity is divested, and a stand of intellect is made righteous. The manner of good following aligns the Savior with the perfect presence of His will and makes a heart of understanding gain with knowledge the unity of Christ Himself with the people of His bride. This is a manner of true courage, and the gift of goodwill ensues. If a plant of light is not heeded, no growth will be administered. How a community or township reflects the love of God is determined by their commitment to Him as a whole. The town of residence a person adheres to is his name of recognition. God is the sponsor of man, and in Christ, we are made as one with His person. The light of the great I Am is ever forthright. The following gift of truth is from God by His witness to our hearts. Boaz spoke for the community he resided in when he followed the presentation of legal affairs that were the custom of his lordship in the manner of faith and support. The knowledge of Jesus had not been made available, yet Jesus was still residing on the throne and in full control of the proceedings. He laid claim to the testimony of the closet kinsman who rejected the offering of kinship to Ruth, and his representation faded out from lack of interest in sharing the wealth of the union. The kinsman of Boaz was sure-footed, and the unity in God was adhered to. When the light of Christ is reflected to a people group, understanding is where truth and support maintain the bond of support represented. The gift of enlightenment is felt when the heart acknowledges the union and receives the knowledge in a fair manner. God is always light and hope. In His manner, truth is subject to the unity of the King, where support is recognized, and the gain is an assembly of the station of God. If following in the way of God is a desire, your representative of people will grow in the offering of light you put forth. Taking into account that some are not following the great I Am labels, one is an administrator of guidance. Taking on the challenge of a committee is not for all who aspire to share the love God holds for them. Writing is one way to gift a friend or person in need with care. A simple note in a person's handwriting opens the gateway for an expression of love to go forward. Simple gestures pour into the heart of a person. All genders, both male and female, learn from one another. If you plant favor to a person, understand God just connected you to him. How the person receives the plant is in his own specifics as to his character and demeanor. A light of good intent will feed the soul of a weary person, given they are open to the gift in its entirety. If a label of division was the goal, a gift would reflect the negative manner, and no unity would be rested within. God operates on a plateau of light, so build in the same way He does. Light the path for many to learn by your example and lean into the knowledge God will grow your favor and support. A witness is always visible in one form or another. Let your appreciation for God be your signature employment in the manner of strength and regard for one another. Each envelope of good intent is a statement that God is superior to all of mankind. He is the one all lean to in order to have growth in the event that a goal of light comes by way of a path where development is not a party of unity; step outside of the claim and make your decision final. A representation of doubt and dark pretense is not a gain but a trap. Leading in the way of light will aspire to the unity of good hope. Favor the light and be in the wise community of faith builders. Align with the God of all and know Him in a personal manner. The gift of unity will act as a whole of good, moral, righteous manners with the pure level of guidance one needs to grow in faith and guidance.

Unity Maker Three

God Is Personable

Righteous mannerisms gift light and important goals ensue.

God the Father is righteous and good. In Him is truth and hope, where all of mankind can know the light of good intent. The lead God offers is wholesome and pure. When operating as a team, grow in the manner of good, moral, and righteous behavior. The unity will project as solid, and the gift of light and hope will unfold.

A team in a marriage unity is one of a constructed way of guidance. The body of light they administer is binding because of a contract where both parties commit their personage to one another. No separation should be visible if God is at the helm and instructing the goal of the bond between them. God offers guidance where hope is at the forefront of the thought process. Just as Boaz was inclined to protect and secure a partnership with Ruth, so should a husband of today adhere to the same principle in the same manner. Being tied as a believer in God reflects the bond and care of love God holds for man and the vision He has for him.

The lineage of Boaz was a way for God to bring forward the reward of His Son to all generations of all time. The light of God is ever available, and the power of His gift of enlightenment is available in many forms. The Bible is found readily on any website offering written material from various authors and leaders of a region. The influence of the Word is reflective in that it never evolves. Care and structure are made viable when the truth is adhered to and represented as the unified presentation of Christ to man. The Bible is the measure by which we are to secure our thought processes. Alignment with the Word of God is insightful and wise.

Actions of study bring clarity and truth to the forefront of our souls. The witness and understanding are right and true. When instruction surfaces, a bond of light is made available to the spirit, and truth builds with hope and favor. The light of God is brilliance and good insight. If you align with the King and the structure of your idea-making is the truth about who the risen King is, then you have found favor and support from God on high. God makes a path where there is none by allowing good fellowship with His person. The alignment He makes visible will adhere to your heart, and a bond of love will be built upon. God at work means movement of growth is on the horizon—plan for strength when you have a vision or an idea of important material witnessing. God operates where He is welcome. When you invite the Lord to take over your cares and your wisdom path, there is the understanding He will attest to your good intent in the manner of favor and righteous gifts. The people who showed contempt for God were lost and unsuccessful in the way of eternal life and unity. God is the one who watches the goals we set in motion, and He is the one to administer our love angle. Bonding with God is an important lifestyle where hope resides and grace is fluent within us.

The power of the great Waymaker is not insignificant. It is unlimited, and it supports the knowledge God is righteous and holy. No other is quite like Him, nor will there ever be. God is more than a planner or investor. He is the gift of unity where He resides with us in a personal way. This tie is binding and good in its formation. The goal of the righteous One is always one of true sponsorship. God authors our minds with a plan where He is the supplier of hope garnered with clear goal-making. If we compare the power of God to that of an individual, we miss the stand of the Almighty. He is greater than all of man combined. He is extensive and whole in the way of grace and support. He encompasses the ground of the entire universe and then some. He has no limits, nor does He inflict any loss on any of His children. Those who choose outside of His person are administering a unity with Satan. They may not believe this is the case, but it is true. We know this from the verse where the daughter-in-law of Naomi, who stepped outside of the coverage Naomi offered, showed a desire for another way of life. The example reflects we all are required to pursue one God, not that of another. We do not read what partook of this other daughter-in-law, but there is no future in her walk as she is not recognized beyond that of favor from Naomi, where Ruth is shown as an administrator of Christ. Her lineage states she was a follower of Jesus even though she didn't know it at the time. Whom we serve is a question only we ourselves can divest in. If we pursue the goal of bonding with God, we will reflect Him in many forms. Whether we choose to follow another form of witness, that too will be understood. However, there is only one true King and that is prophesied all through the Book of light.

God is the benefactor of giving when a heart supports Him in the way of goal setting. The tie of God to man is not one of jeopardy but one of integral hope and fortitude. With God, the light is given where the goal is made manifest and supported as a gain in strength. By the power of God, man is able to relate the purpose of God-given talent, and in the process, a unity is crafted that portrays a binding network of built unity. How this transpires is made viable by the power of the great I Am. He is the one to align a gift of light and to make it a care unit of good intent. God is the Waymaker and in Him is the garnered option of going forward with a gift of light supporting one to another. A stain on the heart is not made a design element when Jesus pursues the union. His blood is a stain remover where unity and a derivative of light abound. By His standard light is portrayed and the real gain is a witness to His person. The offering of God from the Book of strength named Ruth is a gift of good material that structures our union to Christ. It reflects the body and supports the manner of hope God puts forth through His Word of the Bible. Each verse and stand is made understood through prayer and direct communication with God. When we guide our hearts toward the true character Christ portrays, we align with His way of being. Just as was written in the time of Boaz, structure with the great I Am is a purpose and a union none are able to rival.

Take into account the manner of design where God developed the union of Boaz to Ruth, where He shouldered the burden of the crop material for feeding to be claimed as a result of tending the field by the men under the influence of Boaz. Had God not been party to the offering, there would not have been a unified handheld witness from Christ to the people of that generation. How this was granted was by way of lineage and support of God to the people group of strength who in turn supported God as King. The light and knowledge of God were adhered to, and a plant reflective of growth was gifted to the main stand of integrity where God was the leader of the group of people under the guild of the Father Himself. A reflection of truth was present, and the knowledge God is viable in the life of man was adhered to.

God the Father knows how to persuade a goal and make a life-breathing grant of hope. With Him as the mainstay, many are sponsored and raised to the level of hope God gifts with care. A unity of trust and persuasion was not the offering in where doubt resided. The idea of God being a thrust of manners where He lands the heart as a bullhorn is not how He operates. With God, the unity is instructive and supportive. He does not step on the individual's desire for hope or gift-building dreams. God organizes the dream, and He develops it in a form of gifted visual understanding. A unity may form outside of the support you had intended, but with God, all things work toward good for those who love the Lord.

Unity is not without a support measure from God when you apply your heart and goal setting in the way of garnered understanding. This means tying your will to that of God. The offering of knowledge made viable to your reflective conduit of growth is not one of insignificant gain. The work of the Lord is always a viable intent where truth is registered to the heart. The bounty may not reflect the pocketbook, but the goal of God is to unite man to Himself, not to build wealth, so rot and decay can inbreed to it. God sets the goal, and He makes a love offering so many will recognize His support. The detail of strength is not often remembered as a facet of adherence, but without it, no building would ever be made complete. God is the factor of hope that builds within a person when a dream is recognized. Dreams hold wisdom when God is at work in a person's perspective. If the bounty is waged against the dream vision, then the loss will follow suit as with God, the inherited value is His righteous endeavors to the man, not money in the pocketbook. Yes, inheritance can be made a part of the wise counsel, but it should not lay claim to the goal as a whole. Meaning the walk of light should be an invested hope for man to align with the will of the Father. A future of growth will abide when God is the reason for the graft of work intent.

Taking the knowledge of God and pursuing it as a dream in the way of presenting oneself to others is not always comfortable if stepping out in faith brings us out of our comfort zone. Know God works through our estranged manner and builds character through the goal setting. If personal commitment is on the platter of divisive thoughts, recognize God is skilled in operating with the goal of strength. He will make available the drive and the influence, and your support will garner the incentive of strength where hope and a plateau of guidance abound. This is how God operates when a plan is being developed. The goal is for many to gain not just one individual or one singular unit of inspiration. A build where many thrive and contribute is a golden bounty seen as good and standing in the line of gratitude.

When God aligns with us personally, our vision will be as He desires. The body man represents is one of a standard that is not a whole package. So, building in the manner of intent that supports Christ is a better adherence to the truth of the Father and His goal representation. When alignment of God to man forms there is bounty of insight that garners the goal and makes it adhere to the standard of God not man. When man offers a goal, the intent must reflect the drive and the way of the build. Where the projection stands as a whole is what describes it to the heart. Offering fruit is wise counsel and with the gift of knowledge secures the love fest of strength God offers as a resolve where light shines forward to others.

Our intent is the interest of God. He is the mainstay and the divine truth, so He hears our hearts and minds with the knowledge of each detail we have within us. The personal gain of following in the path of light is not one of minimal thought processes. Our hearts reflect the goal of strength with the alignment of guidance only the King is able to build upon. Boaz was light in the manner of operating the land property he held. He reflected as strength when Ruth and Naomi were in need. God made within his person the desire to support the women and to lean into them with care. God operates in this manner. He guides and leads with genuine intent of good wages.

Trust is not gained by simply believing or witnessing others at work for the King. How a person gains in strength is due to the reality God favors his path and gives truth to his spirit. Walking with Christ is where hope builds and lands within the mirror of man's gateway to God. How a man perceives the Lord is representative of unity but not in the manner of a loss or a witness of lies. Man will lead in the path of good intent when he abides in favor of God. When God is the reason man works for unity, a method of hope is made upright. Gain by way of Christ supports others, and it enlightens the heart with care and truth. There is concern when a person leads to quickly or works in a swift manner. Building in unison with God is a viable path forward. If planning is involved, know timing is in the hands of the Father. Expectations that a cure will be made viable in a disease situation is not secure as no one knows God's desire for an individual. Timing reflects the love God holds for all. Unity is forthright when a glimpse into the future presents as a way forward. The timetable of light will adhere to the availability of any person with the groomed intent and the same expression of desire. People unite for an ideal where unity is a graft and a support beam. If no alignment develops there is no recognition to the goal, you put forth. This does not mean something won't develop in the future, but at the time of the intent, there may be hurdles in the way where other gifts are in pursuit of the goal line. Boaz could relate to the people of the community where he subscribed to the goals of the town he partook of. He was an example of light, and he gifted others with support. He followed the manner of law, and he respected the way unity was grafted by the witness he presented. How we manage our goal system is a reflective manner of strife or good intent. Who we patron and serve reflect whether we serve Jesus or the dark one. Satan can influence our decision-making and try to steer us in the direction of self-gaw, where we are consumed with the idea of fame or unity with ourselves.

Look at where Naomi stood when it came to the support of Ruth. She showed favor and gifted love. Unity was a gift she offered by way of marriage to her son. Through the course of time gain was administered and a union of goals united in the way of support one to another. Think about the relationship goals you have with counterparts within the family unit. The makeup of families today is different from the day of Ruth or Naomi. Boaz was a man of hope where; he supported the women and showed them kind favor. In the world we live in, this is not common practice. Offering light is not conducive to gaining in the way of wealth so many fail to offer lodging or vacation stays for unlimited announcement and as a result no one has a free tab. Today, homes are built for family members who reside in the home. There aren't rooms added for the support of visitors as there once was. Sharing hotel expense is a dividend with a tab many can't afford. Arriving in the name of the great manner of wealth is few and far between. Meaning a witness of shame is what presents when someone is unable to maintain the same support as their counterpart. Naomi and Ruth had to trust God would provide for them when they traveled to the homeland once known to Naomi as her family unit and connected bond of help. If you are alone, the bond of God is the strongest unity you could place your trust in. Just as He provided for Naomi, by way of garnering a family tie willing to offer her support, too Christ will support you with a connected bond of strength.

The tides of time are short in today's way of being in relationships of marriage. The way it presented in the days of Naomi and Ruth was no one divorced without first having the reason of adultery to support the division. However, the relationship was still to have respect and support as it was divided. There needed to be a decree stating the transgression and why the marriage ended. Unity was important in the generation leading up to the birth of the Savior. The unity of man to God supports the love man holds in favor of light with hope at the core of the understanding. When a light shines bright, it is a signature God is at work. How reflective the body who engages with its presence is tied to the gift of knowledge. A person who studies the Word of God gains in the manner of solid care where the gain sought after is made a realization because it is the Waymaker in whom favor is gifted from. People miss the unity if they don't seek the counsel of God. He has grafted the knowledge to the pages of the Bible. He has gifted man with the Manual for all things good and bright. The power of God is not an adherence to indignation. The offering of hope from God is a registry of light that no other is gifted in providing. The management of the King is always one of good intent. By the measure of a man is the reflective body of his heart. Sin within the life of a person is not a bounty where truth abides. The goal of the heart should be to reflect the same offering of care God leads us in. God tangles the mind with the truth, and a light of recognition unfolds. The timing of when a person understands the light of His Lord is determined by the individual seeking God and in what form this transpires.

God the Father is a gift in and of Himself. The power of God is ever forthright. God is all-knowing and powerful. In Christ the leadership is favor and meaningful. Look at how the man of Boaz came into being. He was in the bloodline of the Most High. God granted favor to a family where He would be recognized and pursued. The light of the Lord is seen by the individual who favors light and truth. If you are in a righteous manner, you have found the light to be a welcome mat to your heart. The lead of God is for man to know Him and to pursue Him in a relationship where He is viewed as the lead and head of their connected unity.

God is all-knowing, and in Him is the bond of strength where might is not that of muscles and tendons. God's power is a spiritual unity that supports the light of Him to you in a manner of solid recognition so you are tied with might that leads with grace. God is available to anyone who favors Him as their own personal Savior. The light of mankind is not a wholesome way of being. Without the King as the lead in a person's heart, frailty exists. The heart of mankind is weak in that it desires its own way in all mannerisms. The God of mankind knows the steps that always provide light and hope. If you have an ailment know God, the Father has you by way of His person, so you rest in good company where you are protected in a loving manner. There may be hurtful pains or losses, but this is not the desire God had for man. In the flesh, man is not righteous, so God had to pave the way for man to know God in the light. This is the gift of salvation. Man has a tied element of faith within him.

Even the weak believer is able to grasp the great I Am is all-knowing. The man who claims there is no God truly lies to himself, and the content of the lie is made manifest where righteousness no longer resides. Rejecting the favor of unity provided by God is a path of loss, and leadership is not within the person who lays claim to this perspective. Light in the care development is not aligned with disbelief. When God organized man's goal of salvation, He knew many would reject His gift. He gave man free will so he could have his own destination in unity. Satan deceives the man who desires his own path outside the will of the Father—all the while favoring the darkness of doubt. God is all-knowing, and He offers the unity of Himself to the person who supports Him as holy and pure. God is never in doubt as to whom truly loves and pursues Him in faith. Faith builds man's heart, and it aligns the goal of God to man in the way of contented harmony. The favor of unity is right and stands as light where the heart abides in support of the saving power of Christ. There is no gift of light if Christ is not the goal for the heart. Standing in the way of good favor is not something to take lightly. The acceptance of the Savior to the heart of man requires following the path of unity. The tie of God to man invests with grace. It is the glue of the bond and the support beam of hope. Without the power of God, no one can find salvation, so unite in truth and be a faith instrument of care and alignment in power and favor.

God will infiltrate the goal of man, and he will adhere to the prosperous way of life. Timing by way of a gifted support gate is one of hope and prosperity. How this aligns with the King is a manner of guidance where truth is the requisition and design of an imprint from on high. Alignment is not easily claimed when truth is not welcomed. A path of intent requires the unity of care where man gifts his heart to the King in the manner of surrender, not defeat.

God will adhere to man when He is welcomed in the manner of light and hope. God thrives on the unity where He is supported and worshipped. The hour of recognition is at any point in time. Waiting may result in the bond never seeing fruition or acknowledgment. Gain the bounty and dine on the witness God provides through the Word He has planted for man to know Him by. The desire of God is to support man and to enlighten him in the way he should live and think. Favor comes by way of garnishment from God. Working for the unification of God to your person always brings a return of good form. The bank account is one gesture God will enhance if one's faith believes in His good maintenance structure.

God is the gift man desires within. The unity is claimed and adhered to even if profession isn't spoken. The abstract form of unity is set in motion when a person determines who he will pursue. If Satan brings hope by way of recognizing no God exists, then deception has been received and planted as light. The darkness is no longer visible, and light cannot be recognized. A person who favors no God enhances himself to the glory of a leader, where he is the craftsman of unity. The understanding of truth has become diluted, and no unity is adhered to other than that of the deceiver.

Boaz determined for himself God was light and hope. In this determination, a realization that God is the great influencer of righteous ways prevailed. The wisdom of unity was built upon and site in the way of a gifted bond was adhered to. All the family of God pursue Him as the Waymaker. They tie and bind as one with willingness and support. There is a tether of grit where God will not lose the hold He has been accepted within. God the Father crafts and builds with a square no other holds within. This is what sets Him apart from the person of man. God's alignment garnishes the favor He carries for us as individual operatives who pursue Him in the care and honor He deserves. Our recognition to Him as a witness of strength and gain reports the goal of us to Him. God is all-knowing, and in Him is the gain we all require for eternal hope of life ever after. Christ is the unity where all light derives from. Even the breath of a small, individual child is a gift by the hand of the Most High. Our allegiance to God is made viable when we profess God is the all-knowing crafter of all things great and small. God builds with a unity no other has the ability to operate and graft forth. The design element of the heart has been skillfully made viable when God breathed life into it. The available unity is not a mechanism where man to God is present as the spirit must compel forth as an intent where God is the loyal, recognized being of light and hope. If the heart recognizes the truth, but the spirit rejects the union, a loss is brought forward. Uniting to God is an adherence where both unite in the way of desire from God to His child and back to God. Meaning the bond must flow from one to the another in a freewill operation of faith. The gift of light God portrays is a unity that adheres to the mind in care. The love of God to His child is never ending, and this must be the union of man to God as well.

The tie of God is light and not cumbersome. The power of faith is what adheres the mind in favor of God and His Son Jesus Christ. The unity of the Father to man is supplied by way of intent and the fraction of truth which is 100 percent when God is the realization of the gesture. God is the one to perfect the Book of Love, and He made it complete with no errors. The application of trust God adhered to was one of intent where the mind was gifted a bounty of faith and guidance. The minimal unity of man required to know the heart of God is acceptance of His Son, the Lord Jesus. But know just securing your heart with God is not what builds the favor or the alignment where a bond of gifted knowledge is viable. Many who find following Christ unpleasant do not recognize the plant that is needed for growth and hope to prosper. The design of God to man is for developmental gain to lighten the burden of our inherited manner where sin is not something we retain. The study of God's Word guides our heart and mind, and we delve into the structure of truth and the witness of gain unfolds where truth is the mainstay within our hearts. A light is visible when it glows in care with the wind at bay. The tail of God is ever faithful, just as the heart of Him is always set in the way of positive, enhanced learning. The lead of Jesus is one of solid, enhanced manners that are vibrant and holy. The structure of good gifts is a blessed stand God offers man as a result of following Him in faith. Faith alone does not make the bounty adhere to God's prosperous, mental outlook. We must invest in a personal design where we look to the leader with pure intent and love. Our affection is a derivative of good blossoming hope that justifies who the God we serve attends as. The necessary amount of learning is not adjusted by way of volume. How we apply the act of reading is what stands as holy. If we pursue the Lord and believe He is speaking to us with care, we connect with Him, and a relationship is made strong with grace at the helm.

God the caregiver is a gain for man and a solid way of studying the presence of truth as God gifted the heart with instruction even before the Lord was upon the earth. Naomi stood with knowledge and she partook of the unity of Christ not comprehending He was the gain coming through her lineage to the earth to support man as a whole body of His kinsmen. The title of God is Father, and we learn He is ever present within our hearts and minds. The light of hope God offers is not just limited to the power of all who have gold or silver. He is made viable to anyone who believes He is the great I Am. Through the net wealth of support, the Father of man enlightens the mind, and He gains in the way of the gift of love, which brands our hearts with respect toward His person. The design work of God is to make man righteous and holy with a partnership where the love God contains bleeds to the heart of all who pursue Him in faith. God has bounty for the heart and within the gain is the support of gifted insight when trust is part of the connected hope man has to God. The partnership is one of faith, and it maintains unity, so there is never a breakage or loss. Sin can manipulate a hatred or bring to light a developed manner when lust is in the process of consuming man's strength. To avoid this graft, focus on God and let Him be your goal affiliation. The time of unity will allow Christ the visible bond and broaden it to a glow where you act as a body of glory toward the King.

God is the timetable and unifier where support aligns, and goal-making brings a tied respect from a person to the reflective heart of the King. Meaning God is the factor of strength we can adhere to knowing He will always care for us with true commitment and hope where trust is truly made viable. Our way of presenting a relational goal is not always made in the way of a solid unity. Marriage often dissolves because adultery enters the heart and breeds a lie of unity that isn't real in its livelihood. Passion is what enhances the desire, but it is fleeting and there is no real substance to the connection. Over time it will fade, and the bond will dissipate, and the manner of the graft will drive a wedge to the people of the community where the trial of temptation existed. This is what happens when children suffer and form a unity with dark dreams of being made free from the pain inflicted upon them when the divorce becomes a factor in their home life. God's gift of light will not be one of a loss where many are deprived of the unity He supplies. A plan of neglect is not the best for man. A goal of unified hope is what presents as trust and support. A division inflicts a hurt which festers if the salve of God is not placed upon the wound. The man God put in line for the commission of faith was one of integrity and moral righteousness. Boaz was that man in the way of unity and support for the future bride he would couple with. Every detail of the book of harmony called Ruth supports the love God has for women as a whole. The context therein is made viable because God supports all of mankind. This includes the female gender.

God organized the goal of bringing a family into the fold of hope when he offered the gift of marriage to a woman who had lost her unity partner. When death hits the stage of unity, such as a marriage of good standing, there resides a pain inflicted, which brings doubt and anguish until the love of God is enlightened. In the way of Ruth, Naomi had favor as she was aligned in the knowledge God supported her even if the male partners of the family were no longer the lead of the family unit.

God serves all of mankind. Through the unity He provides, our hearts align, and the offering of light comes forward. Support from God to man is viable, and in the bond is the favor of trust. God does not inflict a loss until no option of unity is presented. The decision of leaving God for another will unveil the mind into darkened desires, causing truth to fade and the spirit of the wicked one to infest the goal of the person where all recognized unity dissipates. The favor of God to man is not a small undertaking. You must adhere to a daily provision of where you make the righteous decision to pursue in faith the way of God. Personal commitment is what determines the unity and how far the trust resides. God supplies the bond with His favor, and the light of hope is built with a mainstay where the unity is tied in a tight formation. Strength from on high is magnified and lifted toward the bond when you invite the Savior into your heart. The goal-building aligns, and the present desire for fame fades into a direct truth where you gain knowledge that God is the one to glorify. He alone is the great I Am. No other is righteous or justified. The person of God is always aligned in the way of desiring the truth to be shared and compiled, where faith and unity are the goalposts. Each testimony of the heart represents the manner of the mind, and it entangles the unity of God to the righteous way of gifted expression. The enlightened heart hears the call of the Savior, and it welcomes the Lord to his person. Leading by way of desire is a false pretense, and no claim of victory will unfold. God's tower of life is full of hope and light. He is truth to the core, so know you are in good hands when you embrace the unity He offers.

Christ is the gift of unity, and His personal manner is righteous and good. He makes a way for man to adhere to His person in such a way that light reflects from the heart. The graft of love God desires is for man to work as a unity in the way of friends and family. A business is glory to God when the people who establish the bond of a witness do so with good intent. An operative of the Most High supports growing and gaining but not in the presentation of default. A light of truth must be present for anyone to desire repetitive customer investments. Boaz understood this principle. He acted with respect when the land offer was within his grasp. He did not go outside of the faith he knew reflected God, and he waited on the decision of the closest kinsman. This prevailed as a unified presentation, and the offering was garnered with righteous acceptance. The role of God is our provider. He stands in unity with our hearts and minds where we know right from wrong. How we proceed is our own choosing, but there are consequences to our decision-making. The decision of Boaz to make a better life union for Ruth and her mother-in-law was a determination of good intent. Not all unity binding forms are so secure but the platform you maintain is what sets apart the heart of the faithful to that of a loss in standing. A witness can be tarnished where a path of loss was wandered upon, but know God can make right the graft of darkness. He is able to wash it clean and form a hedge of strength in its place. The power of God is gold in the way of investment for the future of any individual with a purpose and a cause for righteousness. The alignment of God is a stand that supports the body and the heart, so both bend to the will of the Father. The unity of God to man is tied when a person believes in the great I Am as his one and only provider. All other desires fade, and the truth is what reconciles the mind to the heart. A clear understanding is what gains the heart retribution to align in favor of Christ, the one and only King. Life goals build over time, so many form when we are young and impressionable. Our heart discovers darkness as well, and over time, we desire what feeds our spirits. If you find only enlightened guidance from God is what soothes your spirit, you have gained unity and care from God. The favor of Christ is supportive, and with it is the present alignment of man to Him in a personal endeavor. God feeds the person who pursues Him with the intent of righteousness and guidance from the great I Am. The signature of God is freedom in the way of gifted understanding. The alignment of God is not one of an adherence where no gain is permitted. God often brings light and unity in the way of prosperity. His favor is bright and supportive. When a person leads with guidance, a true gain is made comprehensible to others who witness a lifestyle of righteous living. Sales may increase, or notoriety may unfold, but know keeping God at the forefront of your life is what will garner the period of strength where you build with character and recognition to the Most High. God pursues His stand when a relational support measure is adhered to. This means God is the Waymaker, and with this understanding, one operates in unity where God and man tie as partners who express good intent in any relational representation.

Ruth was not alone when she traveled to a new land. God never leaves us or forsakes us. He personally watches over every step we take in His direction. Trusting in the Savior supports knowledge and unity, so you invest with wisdom and guidance where favor comes to you by the hand of the great I Am. Look to unity as a way of expressing your goal front response. You will adhere to truth, and through the walk of intent for good, your authorship will be made visible in the manner of sound expressive hope.

The timetable of the young is not recognized until age sets in as a lump of favor where the body has injuries that fester at times due to wounds that came in the period of childhood. A bounty of favor is when God mends an injury and restores the feeling to a hand or leg. Though not all healing comes in the way of physical manifestations, some require surgical intervention or a doctor's guidance, where support is bent by way of education. Light from the union is knowledge of how to serve the body with a product of medicine or repair measures of exercise which unfold from the hand of God. Either supports the growth of union from an individual of knowledge and one of an embodiment of injury. The injury may be present because of lack of instruction when guidance was given. However, with the great I Am, this does not manifest. God always knows the best advancement to operate from. In Him is light eternal, and by His person, we find comfort. The goal of God for His people is one of unity, not division. So, rest in the knowledge God leads with a kind, instructive gift of unity and care. God offers light, and through His care, man is made viable to have life eternal. When enlightenment is witnessed, the love of the Father is on the platform of strength, and the support is poured forward toward the bond of unity of man to Himself. The love God holds is always an investment where truth and guidance plant. Knowing the Lord underlines the gateway of support, and man dines on the instruction God offers. Christ is the gatekeeper. In Him is found the life-giving unity where care is more abundant than a reel of strength made from iron or rods of steel. God is glorious and wholesome. Trust in Him and know the bond of true, formal gain.

Robin) (Rochel) Arne

Unity Maker Four

God Holds All Things Right and True

God is a creator of the land and the beauty therein.

The light of God is favorable if unity resides within the person who claims God for himself. God entangles the heart with pure intent, so man is able to comprehend good from evil. If the goal of bounty is to know God in a personal manner, hope will infiltrate the mind, and a pure method of operation will manifest. Someone with influence secures the heart when he offers another the goal where the desire for good is expressed. Alone, man is not capable of growing in favor of one another. God must deliver to man the original plan of light in order for there to be light within the heart and mind.

The flow of decision-making is an expression of the desire of the content within the heart. If favor is righteous and in the persona of light, the organized thought process will grow as wisdom, and there will be gain. The person who delivers a guidance of truth will have a representative of hope residing within. This is the great I Am. If you pursue the goal of intent to support, many righteous waves of understanding are within you. Look at how Boaz planned for Ruth in the event she was accepted by another kinsman. Boaz offered the truth in order to bend the will of a man who did not carry the reflective truth of light he possessed.

When God made Adam, He knew he would carry forward without clear intent at all times. That is why he declared man was not to eat of the tree of good and evil. As a result of Adam sinning against God and taking of the tree, he lost the purpose God had placed upon his life, which brought hardship in the way of labor for both Adam and Eve. We ourselves would not have chosen any better, for man has sin within his person. All of mankind would have taken the false expression of the enemy and been led astray. Today, Christ is our witness . All His gifts are light. He has developed the unity with the death of His person at Calvary. The burial and resurrection proved God is above all there is that comes against Him.

He took what Satan meant for evil and made it justified. God knew the plan of the enemy before he did. Alone, this proves God is above all of mankind as man is limited in his ability to have life eternal. It is the bridge of the Most High that enables man to accept the unity and to gain in the manner of faith.

God enables man's gift of himself to be the reflective bounty God desires where a relationship is maintained. The style of our mind is unique to each individual offer we claim as solid or the gift of enlightenment. By pursuing the King, we gain in intent and support. God gifts our love with His flavor of goodness. Through the Love of God, we unite to His person, and we dine on the unity that leads us to the cross, where we meet and tie as partners of light. If the goal you possess is to further the representation of God, know He has purchased your claim and made it secure with His person. God ties the heart and secures it to the unity He designed from His throne of integrity. The light of the King is divine and holy.

God enables the love of man to be a witness to His person. When an offering of light is maintained within our person, we feed off the gift and we are inspired to record the bounty as favorable. The lineage of Jesus was made viable when Boaz accepted the gift of salvation put forward by God before Jesus was born. This is an accepted principle as God and His Son are one. The channel of unity of God to Christ is one of an adherence where there is never a burden or loss. The power of God is enlightening, and through His person, man finds the gift of light. Never doubt the Lord leads in gain and support. He is gold in the form of wisdom and strength. The union of God to man is forthright when we bind to the gift of light and believe in the connection as unending. The table of life is ever righteous in the manner of understanding as God offers knowledge to all of mankind. He is not inherited or deranged. By the reflective way God portrays the love He possesses for man, we witness the grace and gift of truth as a witness in the manner of integral hope. God supports man by way of His Son in the righteous gift of light that is incarnate. The holy cross was not just a death sentence. It was a mandate for the blood of the Lamb to fray the edge of loss so man could gain entry to the truth and receive care that abounds by way of forgiveness and repentance. The two meet and a divide is sealed where man has knowledge of who the Master of all is.

When unity is a desire, a fountain of hope retains the ministry, and wealth flows forth. The power of God is unique, and there is none more righteous or holy. The great I Am is ever upright and good where man is not complete without the unity of God. We gain when Christ is our lead and support measure. The opportunity to claim the seal of life eternal is ever before the heart of man. The Lord is the fountain and support beam that adheres the heart and mind in correlation to the light of God's unity. The manor of love is what brings a heart to the forefront of gain to monitor the truth and proclaim it as righteous. God offers to man a unity of light and hope, supporting the math of good intent. How this reflects to the burden of growth God brings to the table is one of significant mannerisms. There is truth in the way of guidance, and there is a reflection of adhering truth when a person invests in the light of the King. The shield of God is always aligned within the parameter of righteous ways. Binding by way of instruction is a solid way to operate and build. If a plan of light is your goal, you are working for the love of the people in your region. The goal of God is to plant man in favor of light, where hope builds and grafts to the spirit. The desire of man to know Christ is within his person. A map of guidance is only as good as the supplier of the guidance system. If the light is your union maker, then God is at work, making you justified and whole. The time of light being made viable is one of understanding where man learns and favors the will of the Father.

God builds with a union where hope and faith are partners. The plan from God is a brilliant way of presenting a gifted light claiming the King's way of presence. Leading in the manner of tithe and respect is a sure-footed gift of understanding. Man does not tie the heart to the Savior if he is not willing to gift to God in return for his labor. Growing in cash flow supports the mind where trust forms according to the bounty of the bank account. However, a bank account is not security when it comes to health or desires of the heart. You can't make another person love or cherish you for all time. God is able to be that secure being. He will always love and honor you if you have chosen Him as your Lord. Even the people who live outside of His person with no communication in His direction are still loved by Jesus. How this presents is separate from the birth of man to God, where salvation has transpired. The salvation gift is an accepted bond between God and man, allowing for the unity of a relationship to be present and for light within it to shine. How God the Father designed this unity is beyond anything man is able to create or manufacture. Time is a factor when there is little hope of future days. An elderly person leans into God in a more favorable manner. He will adhere with a willing heart as death is close to his lifestyle. Death brings to light either eternal gain or loss by way of no kinship with God. God is all things bright and unified. If you believe you can reside in hell with favor, you are believing a lie of the dark one. There is no hope in hell, nor is there any presence of unification. Your friends won't be at your side, nor will an angel of light appear. There will be wailing and gnashing of teeth for all time. The God of man is light, gifting, and wholesome. In Him is the gift of eternal hope, and all things align in favor of unity. People who support the love God holds are garnered to Him in faith. The bond is irrevocable. No person in heaven will ever desire to walk upon the path of loss.

The goal of man to Christ is for there to be a stand of light and good favor. Building with God is supportive and favorable to that of light upon the recognized heart where no loss is ever felt. There will be no death or tying of favor toward a false pretense as with God all things are righteous. When a person desires to be one with God, they bind their desires toward Him in the way of a unified bounty. This is the claim of Christ to our lighted path of eternal witness. God offers to man the justified reaction of hope so as to claim truth for all time in the form of knowing the great I Am in a personal relationship.

Naomi was a follower of Christ before she knew Him as Savior. God has granted man the knowledge He is real, and by this unity, we are made complete. Naomi understood the truth of God, and she claimed Him as her Lord and guidance counselor. The light from God to Naomi was a guarantee she would know the Son when death claimed her to the grave. A resurrection of hope was within her mind and spirit. She recognized God was who He claimed to be and through the connected manner of her trust a tie was crafted, and a bond of righteous living was her forefront way of presenting her lifestyle which speaks to the fact she knew the Lord before His birth. God and Jesus are tied as one, so she was grafted to the Savior in unity while knowing the Father in a personal manner. Walking in faith is the necessary unity of adherence required for man to trust and hope in Christ alone as his Savior. Whether you believe in the King or just the Father is what determines your path in the lighted form of bonding where truth is recognized and received for the good of the heart. God is the unity for man to live by, but knowing Jesus in a personal relationship is what cements the love of God to the power of His name through the acceptance of the saving power made available by the Son Jesus. The two are one, so one must believe and accept both to be a witness of unity where light is solid and burdened in the way of representation of good form and trust. God targets the bond of light, and by way of His guidance, we learn and decipher the truth of Christ and His plan for our lives. Through this offering, our lifestyle will adhere to the knowledge we hold and believe in. God is the bounty and the torch of guidance, so we are able to learn and develop in the way of light. God supports man, and He leads him with care. God claims our unity, and through His offering of faith, we lean into the knowledge He is all-powerful and forthright.

God crafts in the way of truth, where the dream of man will align with the option of growth supporting the love of God. God aligns the will of man with His person, and a bounty of good unfolds. The declaration of unity is crafted by the Father alone. He is able to withstand a loss or impoverished intent because He is the great I Am, an all-knowing and perceiving gift of light. God furnishes man with growth, allowing a forefront of strength where faith is tied to the goal of an engineer. Meaning God is all powerful with a bind of glue surplusing the heart with a stand of intent where truth is supported and maintained. God breeds unity to align the mind in the direct path of instruction adhering the frontal manner of care where truth and support are tied together in relief. The goal of God is for all of mankind to align with His will, resulting in a unified way of being. God, the all-knowing force of enlightenment, is not hollow or of a lost nature. By His representation, our heart is made in the image of His person.

The structure of God to man is not one of loss but of gain. The way of interpretation in the form of truth is what gifts the heart with instruction and guidance in the manner of unity. God alone is the one to build in unison with Christ, but we, too, are able to bring life-giving testimony to another. Our example of living in the care and support of the Savior is a guidance measure found through the discipline of knowing the King. It comes by way of reading with structure in the Word of the Lord. Each detail of the Bible holds the bounty of good understanding. A pathway of trust is what determines our message of light to others. The structure of good faith is a unity providing support and a lineage of favor with the tie of favor from God. To understand the way to proceed with a goal is a talent the Lord grants when the tie of trust is made viable. If you look to where Ruth placed her heart, you will adhere to the gain God made viable through her. The unity of God to Ruth was the gift of a marriage where love was abundant and hope was presented in faith. The lining of favor from God to her person was of grace and support.

The realization that God supports man is not always comprehended or utilized. If you have a dream but no unity of the Father, you will wait and not pursue the goal He planted. If a pathway is presented and you desire the step, then trust the Lord has prospered you in the way of support. A bounty of strength will adhere to your person, and you will find truth is aligned with character where you grow and prosper in opportunity. Reaching out to others is a way to make your plan recognized and adhered to. If a timetable presents as too long, invest in the option of a new platform. The alignment may be supported in a new form, and the light of governing may arise in a character plan that entangles the heart and mind. Look at the available growth for your goal and seek wise counsel as to how to make it viable. If others do not support the goal in your care, turn away from the vision quest and pursue another form of victory where you stand unified with favor. An availability is not a platform that stands on its own. Favor of God places the truth of maintenance in accordance with the projected income. Knowing the goal and how to make it stand is the way in which Christ delivers a truth. He garners the option and releases the goal in the way of support that leads to the bond of strength, so light shines and forms a barrier of truth. Boaz held property where many relied on him for gain. He did not step forward to obtain Ruth's parcel without first understanding the available kinsman's lead. He stood at the ready to operate with faith, but only if the door of opportunity was made viable.

The operating way of God is to maintain a source of guard where the heart and mind are tied in unity. When comprehending the light, a path forms when the goal is witnessed as a unity. The support of God to man is not of a small endeavor. God leads with a purpose and a path of strength. Knowing God will provide is not the only viable way of approaching the unity structure of a build. The call to your heart must be heard in such a way that your goal aligns with ability and desire. If you suspect an influence of doubt has entered the scene, read the source of good food to the spirit. The Bible contains the unity graft you need to adhere to the will of God. Investing just to make something happen is not wise counsel. It does not stand as a witness of favor, nor does it support the heart when loss ensues. Each support measure must realize the goal as a whole. It needs to be registered in the way of good intent along with the viable, mental stand of strength. The unity God has toward a goal will align with a viable gift of enlightened, available gain. You will find favor and support, and your needs will graft as complete, not a gaping hole of loss. Investing all you own is not wise counsel, no matter how grand the display of strength may appear. Losses do arise and there needs to be a way of growth when honest business dealings fall victim to theft as a result of unsure, retired thought processes. Look at the manner of support Boaz had when he gained Ruth's property. It was not a hardship for him to keep her title on the deed. The property had a reserve where Boaz was plentiful with his own inheritance of unified purchases from prior standing in faith with God at the helm of his life.

Working with the goal of care is what sets apart a dream from a true connection of God. If you have a stand where your goal is not viable, wait for the truth of the present need to come forward. A build in the way of support will land on the platform of genuine grace, and a bounty of favor will come forward. God operates with unity as his goal, so know he never moves unless the timing is accurate and squarely in the right frame of pursuit. Align your thought process with true character and wait on the Lord to gift you with understanding. The timetable may not be correct, so trust God to provide during the drought. A stack of goodwill does not favor itself, just as a build done in a rushed manner does not make for a sturdy foundation.

Work aligns when there is structure and guidance for many to bind in the secure knowledge God is the builder and grafter of light. A unified hope is one of strength, and the tie of unity is solid with moral righteousness. Knowing the will of the Father takes care and prayer support. God crafts with the knowledge of the all-knowing being. He makes things come alive, and through His way of being, much favor brings forth unity. A tie of support from the hand of God lasts for all eternity, so gamble on His bond and know that structure is what sets apart a build from God to that of the devil. When Satan offers a dream, it is to cause havoc. His desire is to make man lose heart and to stumble away from the truth of the King. Trusting God brings unity and support. The will of God is always a place of support and favor. If you stand alone in your goal, you have not found the landing pad of unity. Trust God to build with you, and let Him be the one to provide the open doorway. In the wait, you will find a calm where truth and guidance rest.

The light of mankind does not adhere to the favor of the Most High. The aptitude of man is small in comparison to Christ. God's light grows and shines with support, and the truth of the Word will adhere to the desire. A gain of strength supports the will of the Father, and a manner of good truth will be viable in the actions put forth. Knowing the aligned will of God is something all of mankind desires to gain. Lean into the Word and let the wise counsel come forward. The page of the written contents will adjust your perspective, and you will gain unity and care. God builds by way of His wise counsel and through the adhesion a mind gathers the instruction needed to aspire forth toward the bond of light God will offer. The timing of understanding the process of truth may not reflect your own desire, but it will be the wise hope of God. Trusting the Lord is what sets in motion the gift of unity, and it plants the favor from above. Knowing the King is the one who provides for all of mankind brings the bond of enlightenment where the Father to the Son is grafted. We are children of the Most High, so we, too, are tied in harmony with the God of all. Our leadership needs to reflect the favor and support of wise counsel. Stepping into the fire just to make a plan come to life is not the way of unity where trust is planted. Timing is critical, and knowing when to leap is what determines the unity of God to man. If no doorway of gain is viable, wait for the action of Christ to take form. Building steps one at a time is what plants the options of growth. We manufacture good intent when we pursue the Lord and bind to His gain. His lead grants to our heart the tie we need to stand in the difference of the darkness that hinders the mind when Satan attempts to lead us from the purpose God has aligned to our heart. When the unity of God to man is understood, a pathway of guidance is viable. God makes a unity carved into the man who trusts His person so know if you are relishing in the favor God put forth you have found the intent of God's purpose for you. Waiting comes by way of favor and support. Timing is that of good truth, so acting in support of a true character promise is the plan of God. Building with a body brings to the forefront a plan where several find hope and growth. Trust the will of the Father and know he operates with genuine support and goal setting in where the unity is gifted, and the structure is wise.

God is the lead in your desire. He stakes a claim to the gift you hold within your person. If a goal has been made viable within you and you recognize a pathway but have no clarity, you are being guided in the wait. Trust the growth in a new manner and let the Lord develop you as a precision, invested tool that aligns with His goal setting. The timetable will come to fruition, and a truth of clear intent will unravel. There will be an adhesive gift of trust, and you will have the unity to move forward. Your desire will have legs, and the truth of goal setting will align with many. You will have aid, and the dream will meet approval and strength with the favor of trust will manifest and guide your talent. You will know where to proceed, and a bounty will stand in a viable way.

God obtains favor from a person who trusts His lead. The truth of the bond is made right when hope is what secures the righteous guidance. The unity of God to man is one of intent where man and God act as one. The lead of God is always supportive, and it offers man trust with care. Building in the way of a great stand requires alignment and gain to be made viable. Trusting the Lord is a skill man must invest in. Knowing when to stand on an issue is what gifts the heart with the true intent of guidance where both it and God reflect in unity. God offers the light and the hope. Through His goal plant much favor aligns and builds. Knowing the will of God is always made viable with the intent of supporting guidance that is forthright and true. Knowledge of God is where support derives from. Reading the Word of God is how man gains instruction and how he obtains favor. The gift of the Bible is how man builds a connection to the Most High. It is what makes man ready to receive the power God has available to the heart. Working in favor of God is a gift of the spirit. Trust builds when man reads the Word and hearing God's voice is what sets in motion the light of knowing the great I Am. The secret manner of care is no mystery. It is declared above heaven and earth by every gift of light bestowed upon man. Our minds see beauty on a daily basis. God makes viable understandings that He created every person in a unique way and crafted man to know Him personally. As a result, we tie to God in spirit, and we support Him with favor when we bend a knee and pray toward His person.

The reflective gift of a unified understanding does not mean one will not face trials. It is a factor of life that man will suffer in some form or another. The fall of Adam and Eve is a definition of this. We all would have succumbed to the temptation of good and evil that both Adam and Eve fell to. Christ the Lord is ever powerful and fruit-bearing. His person of interest is solid and forthright. His goal is for all of mankind to lavish to His heart their love and good care. Following by way of leadership is a gift of recognized support that tied Ruth to the man of Boaz. He was a staple in the way he held fast to the true witness of kinship. Not all of mankind favors the unity of God. Some prefer to step outside of the care God provides. They fall prey to the belief God is not all-knowing in the way of righteous manners and wisdom. God is light, and in Him is the path of hope where gifted gain is supplied. If you walk in the light and pursue the gift of unity, you will have the stand of a mighty warrior who carries the gift of understanding with clear unity and guidance. Knowing who is speaking to you in a personal manner is what separates the wheat from the tares. Faith binds the heart, and with the connection it provides, favor is bestowed, and an action of unity is cemented upon man. The care of God is not unjustified. God is light, and He is ever unified in the way of support, so trusting in Him is wise counsel.

Boaz was an individual who believed in the Father, and he understood the righteous gift of care God granted him in the way of providing for two women in need. When the light of God is enhanced, the heart relates to the purpose before it. The recognition aligns with the will of the Father, and fruit comes forth. Tying this kind of love shows worth, and the willingness of a person to attend to the will of the Father is what brings forward the bond of love and hope. Following the will of God brings truth to the gate, and a path of good intent unveils in the way of inspiration. Think about the Lord as a spear of trust binding the goal of great influence in the way of gifted talent and guidance. Know the King is ever willing to grant a life of favor when one leans into Him as Lord. Righteous ways happen by way of instruction from the Word of the Father. He aligned His gift of knowledge with His own being, so in the unity upon reading, a solid connection is written upon the heart. Look at how the representation of God to man played out in the life of Boaz. He stood in favor of purchasing the land Ruth had in her control. He did not lose by way of the marriage as he found favor from God above. The property remained in the authorship of Ruth, but Boaz reaped in the manner of a wife, and a gift of a baby came from the union. Knowing God is a gem in the heart. It incorporates the love God has and aligns the spirit with the goal of aid that sets apart the love of man to self to that of another. Divide the Scriptures and let truth adhere to your spirit. The reward will offer a love of growth, and you will dine on the unity.

Supporting man to God is a network of favor when a body of faith leans into the goal of light one to another. If a bounty is on the stage with no understanding of how it is to be made viable, give the unity to God. He will manifest the desire, and a way forward will ensue. Time is irrelevant to the Lord. He operates with care and support, and this is the light He will adhere to. Know timing to man is not in the way of knowing all the angles to a situation. God is the structure of solid unity and by His person purpose is made righteous. If you favor the will of God, plant in your being the tie of grace and let God represent the way ahead. Dine on the unity and stand as a witness with strength. Offer in the wait a goal of bounty where you invest in the truth and offer it to many. How this is made viable in your life is set with the hand of God. Timing brings clarity, and righteous acts of love abound. Favor from the Lord is a gift in and of itself. No one is ever in the dark if leadership in trust is made present in faith and support. God leads with purpose, and His righteous manner is known by the Word He made available to all mankind. It is freely offered when the investment of the Book has been applied but the wisdom it holds is viable only when man invests and reads for himself, then the unity takes shape within.

The gift of hope from the Father is balance and harmony in the form of instruction and adherence by way of the Holy Spirit and His support to the heart. The rice content of knowing the leadership harmony is white as snow with light at its core. To love the truth is a gift of insight offered from the hand of God. He organizes the lead, and by His person, much favor is made viable. Knowing how to pursue the King is a determined lead in unity. Trusting the Lord is knowledge and through the gift of unity favor is bestowed. Look at the manner of gifted wisdom Naomi had concerning how to arrange a marriage where both parties had the desire to unite. Ruth heard the wise counsel and connected with the man Naomi entrusted her to respond to. Ruth was a woman who had no insight before Naomi reached out and offered the knowledge she contained within her heart and mind.

Staying quiet when you have gain for another is not a choice of good intent. Leading in the way of trust is what determines our minds and hearts as to how they invest in others. Our principal way of being is a gift where hope resides. How we apply our heart to the connection of God is what determines our unity with Him. Offering another the goal of bonding and harmony is light in the way of strength. Giving another the option of gain is a support measure that ties the heart to the love of the King. The power of God is one of favor and hope. Through the lead of Jesus, we find favor and growth. The love of man to himself is not a solid witness, nor is it righteous. God makes available talents and gifts where offering others a wise word of guidance adheres the mind to the bond of God and places the heart at the door of good intent. Unity from others is a gift of shared influence, and the spirit of God is available in both regions of unity.

The design measure of love from God to man is not a required team of strength but a guidance way of being. If you lead in the way of available ties in the form of knowledge but have no desire to teach, you are justified in the work when you offer wise counsel by way of understanding if questions arise in simple conversation. Offering all of your traits is not the goal. Simple direction is a leverage that adheres to the grace of God, and it portrays as righteous and good. People share their talent when they offer the knowledge with support, not full leadership. There is a bond of adherence if the secure manner of intent is a witness. A righteous way of presenting is also standing in support. Showing favor by being supportive of the talent you share is one manner of grafting the goal in a forward motion.

Righteous thoughts are good intent. Learning in wisdom and prosperity aren't always in the form of knowledge of bank accounts. God aligns the will of the people by way of understanding that gifts the heart and mind with a goal of tied interests. Building for many has wise standing where the heart graces the thought process with clear insight abiding in truth. Solid options form when a united manner is upon the stage of interest. If a door remains closed, look to the account measure being applied. Is there a stand where a loose foundation is not stable? Should the hour of need arrive a structure with no adherence in the Most High will fall, and losses will ensue. Timing of the Father is not a harsh representation but that of righteous growth. Knowing the needs of many can bring with it a clear, divine knowledge of where to plant the goal of intent. People in need are reflective in the approach, and sure-footedness is a statement of faith where the design element is made viable. Taking wise steps brings labor to a minimum so the balance of strength is not overcome by the hardship of a struggle. The knowledge God has supplied the unity is what makes a stance solid in its representation. Know the Lord never advances if alignment is not in place. Timing to man is a value God sees but does not require. A stand of intent is what is deemed purposeful and holy. If many are willing to stand in righteous manners, a plan will unfold, and unity will be adhered to.

God's work is a gift through the Lord. Boaz recognized the saving power of a unity with the woman Ruth. The gift of love she provided was that of a yearling, as she had no children yet by another man. To Christ, purity is a stand of righteous hood. This is not to say children tarnish the body or are not of importance should a marriage not withstand over time. A child is always precious in the eyes of the Lord and should be in the eyes of man. Each witness is a statement in one form or another. Christ supports all of mankind. Through His person, man is gifted the unity of life eternal. How we offer our heart and mind is favored by the Most High as it determines our unity with Him. Knowing the Lord is a favor of light, which builds the bond and organizes the thought processes. God's care is a sufficient blend of truth and guidance where all of our mind is consumed with His good purpose. Bonding in favor of growth where Christ is the glorified one is what sets apart a heart of truth from one of fantasy. Only God is righteous and holy. In Him alone is man able to gain by way of the cross. Jesus invested His body and His spirit when He hung on Calvary's stand of light. Know the King is always a way ahead and place your favor toward His goal of tied harmony.

God shows man how to operate when you learn what He aids in the way of intent. The Bible holds all the wisdom and guidance a person needs to know for the way of life. The bread of God supports the unity and ties it with support. Only God can enable a growth where man no longer adheres to the dark enabling manner, but he leans into the good of God. Knowing the will of the Father is found by reading the Book of Love. A station where truth is always at the helm is a gain man needs at all times. The strength of the bond between man and God increases when application of the gift of light is connected allowing God the entry to man's spirit which in turn sets in motion the gift of understanding. The power of God is released, and a unity of trust is formed. The bond is spiritual and glorifying to the spirit of God. God is a manager of the hope that manifests in the heart, guiding it to the place of gifted light. The power of God is forthright and holy. Wisdom is favor from God, and it adheres to the soul when the body follows suit. Actions of intent are a path of gain in one form or another. The person who pursues the will of God finds unity and light. The individual who aligns with darkness loses the bond of God to himself. Light is the measure of a man's strength and his own presentation of hope. Leading in the favor of support to the King is a goal that emits a length of good form. Acceptance of the Lord is righteous and good. In the way of integrity comes the shield of faith. It supports man when trials of despair enter the heart. Man will always have interference from the leader of the dark side, but know he has no power over God or you. Recognizing the Lord is a stand of spiritual guidance. It is placed within the heart, and the name of Christ is adhered to in the manner of support from God to man. The alignment builds character and unity with a grace statement of integrity. God is all-knowing, and He aids the mind with the thought process of good intent. A hollow transformation does not build in strength, nor does it bind the spirit. If you are in need of unity with the King, look at the example found by way of Scripture.

16 For God so loved the world that he gave his one and only Son, that whoever believes in him shall not perish but have eternal life. 17 For God did not send his Son into the world to condemn the world, but to save the world through him. John 3:16-17 NIV

Jesus spoke often about the secure gift of salvation. Through the knowledge offered by God, man gains in the way of gifted hope. The power of God is favorable in the way of true intent that supports a heart and feeds it love. Knowing the path of light is a care measure in line with the hope Christ is all-knowing and enlightening. Our Savior never leaves the side of anyone who accepts the truth of the cross. The unity of God through the gift of salvation was built upon the wages of death. The bond of light God witnessed from the people who worshiped Jesus in the day of the crucifixion was made viable when the blood of the Lamb poured down. The Table of Hope centered on unity, and man gained the perspective of light.

Following Jesus in the day of Pentecost was also a righteous way of being. Favor from the King is a support beam, and it stands in unity and goal-making where man and God are tied in faith. Without the grace factor, man would remain lost for all time. The grace covering is the shadow of bond material that grants favor and support by way of trust and unity. Both the women of the study of Ruth understood the Lord was a viable way of standing. Naomi instructed Ruth and taught her to follow the Lord in light of His commitment to her by way of her lifestyle. We ourselves can follow suit and gain by way of the knowledge of the women of the study. Both reflect the tithe of hope and in it is made holy and secure the purchase price. God alone is the great I Am. By Him, we find favor and truth. Without Him, there is no incentive to live righteously, as death would not be recognized. The ministry of the Father is wholesome and favoring, whereas the dark interpreter of time loses life eternal. Satan will not see daybreak once he has been thrown into the lake of fire. All evil will cease to exist, and only the righteous will know hope.

God has a skill set where the love of man is always on His mind. Each person is known to Him in the fact He is the great I Am. No other is able to assume each person's thoughts and witness of the heart. If you have a bond with another, you relate to the manner of love and provision. Our childlike faith will grant us a home with the Lord if we have repented and sought forgiveness. Redemption is a factor of truth when the love of God is at work within your spirit. The lead of others is hope when God is the focal point, and He is the way ahead. Building a structure takes time. Knowing the Lord is at work making a clean barrier of protection secures our heart and mind in the manner of unity.

The temptation to move forward without a plan is not a wise process to pursue. Follow the light and know the love God has in store. If time is a factor, remember the age of man is not what God tabulates on his schedule. He hears the heart and knows the lead it favors. A righteous man gains an inheritance when he makes just decisions and walks in faith. The power of God supports the time frame, so knowing the call is what sets the stage for unity. Stand in support of God's manner and issue the call to His person, making a claim of truth that God is larger in knowledge than any person, man, or animal.

The knowledge of man to God is limited. We need the care of God and His manner of intent in order to thrive or grow spiritually. All the money in the world will not fill the void of the doubt when God is not the reason for the strength you adhere to. Allow the time of growth God offers to reflect the unity you graft to. The great I Am is all-knowing, and in Him is the favor of light, so investing in His way of being is wise adherence. Guarding the mind against the influence of doubt and discouragement is a plan of wise counsel. The maintenance of God is favor by way of reading the Bible. In the Book of Knowledge, one builds in care and unity. The favor of God is unveiled, and true spiritual adherence is made prosperous. Our connection to the King is what determines our growth and our building ability. If you favor the support and hope of God's wise leadership, stand in the presence of His being. Lean into Him with favor and support through prayer and guided counsel study. God will supply the term length, and you will adhere to it willingly. Thoughts will subside, and you will gain in a manner of hope, all the while building in support of the goal. If God has gifted you with a skill and you have offered it to Him in a personal manner, know He has not forgotten you, nor will he. Stand in honor of His decision-making and trust He has you safe in the wait. The timetable is not in your control when you release the favor and trust the lead of Christ. This is a freeing way to operate, and it supports the Lord in unity with a presence of justified hope.

The will of the Father is forthright and pure. Knowing the King is a gain in companionship. The harvest it witnesses is righteous and good. God is ever available, and He binds His favor to your person. Look at the manner of faith Naomi presented when she was put in the situation of no provider. She stood strong and moved to the homefield of her family where favor was granted. Alignment of God to the heart is ever made righteous when truth is at the helm of the decision-making. Family is tied by way of favor, along with the unity of God to the heart. The saving power of righteous living is a way ahead to gain favor and support. Leading in the way of support is the gift of true strength where support resides and stands in bounty. Jesus was united to the gain of the women in favor and guidance. He led them both with true intent. Once they were in the care of Boaz, a justified leadership maintained their hearts and fed their physical bodies with whole, scriptural gain. Knowing the witness of God is important and supportive to mankind. The goal of gain is made viable and holy when the people who are working to unify a people group adhere to the Word of God and favor it as righteousness.

Robin) (Rochel) Arne

Unity Maker Five

God builds With Righteous Work

The righteous way of God is to make a path of bounty for men who trust His ways.

Favor is a gift of enlightenment and a sole supporter of kind will and intent. Meaning the God of all is a statement of true character. He alone is able to transform a city into a path of light where the people group adheres to the promise of the King. By the power of God, many find unity when prayer meets the plan of authorship. If you feel responsible to pray for a group of others where no understanding is guiding them, know you may be an example simply by way of standing for Christ. Take a look at the way Naomi trusted in Boaz as the kinsman redeemer. She did not hesitate to share her knowledge of how to bring forward a union with the Savior through the marriage of unity she inspired. Her instruction was wise counsel, and she stood in support of the growth of her daughter-in-law. She invested her heart and led with support to the gain of both she and Ruth. The leadership was a witness to Boaz, and he obtained a bond of strength where he inherited a bounty of good through the gift of grace. God the Father was instrumental in the retrieval of a household of a fellow bondsman when Ruth offered her structure of wisdom by planting herself on the threshing room floor. She tied herself to the kinsman redeemer simply by standing in unity with Naomi. She acted according to the manner expressed to her person and, as a result, was gifted the love of God in the process. Naomi stood as a representative of care while obtaining a grace of support in the action. God delivered both women to the altar of gain, and He made a living hope pour forth.

God hinders a goal if people aren't accepting of His will. He stands in regard to their concerns and beliefs, and He places the new content of the mission in new surroundings. The stance of true witnessing is righteous and holds merit in the way of truth being the objective. If you have hoped for a path to pursue, but no unity is on the table, walk forward to a new harvest point. The lead will adhere in unity with God, and another plan will build and become the focal point. Leading by way of faith is the garnishment where man and God operate together so a permanent design of strength unfolds. Allowing the purpose of the plan to unfold is a stance of good knowledge and care. The method of unity will be made apparent, and the gain will advance with clear knowledge leading the way ahead.

Christ is an example to follow and pursue. In Him is the gain we all need and require for faith to be present within us. God is all-knowing, and He invests with purpose when we align our spirit to His. The available strength of the King is gifted when we abide with the offering of true ownership. We belong to the Savior as His children of light. Accepting God as the true purpose for our hearts and minds is what determines the path of growth and the way ahead. Binding in favor of light is the unity God designed for all mankind. A look at where favor was gifted to the man of Boaz shows the grace and hope God had for His people. Boaz worked in the field even alongside that of the servants. He was not one to shine his reputation or flaunt His ownership upon the less fortunate. God gifted him with truth, and He supported the gain of Boaz in the way of providing him with marital knowledge in conjunction with the truth of leadership pointing to the body of God. His respect toward the people he governed was representative to Christ and the leadership he portrayed. Knowledge is all meaningful when Christ is the purpose of your heart. Without God, there is only a drive for cash where death waits with greed and corruption. Look at the name of Ruth and remember she had understanding that led to favor and righteous mannerisms. Think about the care and unified way Christ applied the guard of faith to her person. Recognize God can do the same in your life and know He enjoys blessing His people who stand for righteousness and truth.

God speaks to man, and when He offers a word, bend your heart and lean into the truth, knowing the lead of God is forthright. Plant your goal-making in the name of Jesus and build in the way of organized hope that represents the truth of the Word of God. Tying the hand of the Savior happens when one walks slightly on the outside of the structure God built upon. His Son is the representation we are to unite to. Nothing else adheres as the Father to the Son, so in the unification of man to God, Jesus must be the focal point. Leadership is tied by the saving power of Jesus and His death at Calvary. The resurrection stands complete and in the name of Jesus favor is bestowed to man. The alignment is righteous and holy. Trust the leadership of Jesus and build in unity with the goal of God. Knowing the light makes viable the plan ahead. There is unity only if Christ is the way for truth to be revealed. Man believes according to his desires. If he pursues the love of God, bounty brings a haven of gifted understanding. Truth is the ministry and guidance platform that connects the heart to God. God operates with truth at the core of all He builds. He is righteous and holy, always working in our favor. Tie the truth of the Word and bind the Scripture to your spirit. In doing this formula, an inheritance will unfold. You will connect with the Lord on high, and a sanctity will adhere to your person. God is a witness to all you offer another, so claim for yourself the truth and be righteous in the way you operate. The knowledge of truth will be a welcome mat to the weary, and you will adhere to the will of the Father. People of the knowing God are bound in favor, and truth is with them. If the light draws you in and you dine on the unity of God to your person, there is a bond of righteousness permitting growth and the desire to claim Christ as Savior. Acting in the will of God is what sets man in the path of light and hope. Knowing and adhering to the Word of God is a waystation of unity where hope resides and favor is supported.

The structure of unity is a binding form of faith where two meet as one. The guidance measure of support is a gift of faith that adheres to the will of Christ and presents as light to the spirit. God masters the love of man to His united hand of mercy, and favor erupts in the way of a commitment of care. God is not valid in your life if you fail to trust Him with all you are. The path of light garners the mind, and a person of integrity binds to the love offering. God evaluates the mind and knows the thought process taking form within.

A bounty of strength is recognized when a person leaves the fold of doubt for the witness of truth. The elevated bond then grows more adhering, and favor is supportive of the union. The light God presents is unified and righteous in its stand. God does not offer a doubt or a loss. He is an example of gifted love and freedom. With God, there are righteous manners with good intent. All the while, both act as leverage where truth is born and garnered to the heart. God is a magnet, and no other can compare in the spirit of recognition. The optimism of unity is what man correlates to and desires to operate with. The bounty of God is forthright, and one dines on purity if God is the way they operate and blend with Christ Jesus.

A look at the way Boaz presented Ruth to the kinsman closest to her in lineage proves trust was his purchase in life. He gained when he made her stand upright and pure, with the objective being an inheritance that would lead her to security. The name of Ruth is now recorded in the Book of Love called the Witness Manual. God has secured for Ruth the notoriety of a queen, and her story is spread far and wide. The favor of God is always a viable stand, and it reflects trust. The person of God is never unholy, so purchasing His Son by way of admittance and repentance is righteous with care as a backdrop.

God's call to man is a signature of favor designed to adhere to the truth of the spirit. The bond of God with His children is one of strength and support by way of the cross and bloodshed at Calvary. Understanding the truth of such a claim is a gain and inward witness that God is who He claims to be. Any doubt will not withstand itself when the application of faith presents the truth. A simple test of faith will build in accordance with the trust of man to God, and unity will manifest and bloom. Look to the witness offered by way of Naomi and her expressed way of belief. She went forward toward the union offered to her in hindsight, which brought forth the will of God to her person. The knowledge of God and her family presented Naomi with the understanding she would be cared for in her homeland and heritage farm. She was not a landowner where her titled name was written on a ledger sheet, though there was land available through a kinsman redeemer, but with God, Naomi held the name of Christ within her. The staple of unity was present, and the knowledge of hope was laid clear upon her heart.

God works with clear intent, and he operates with structure and guidance. God the Father is righteous and holy. By His person, man is made complete, and in the unity of the two, much favor is witnessed. Offering the light of the Lord is a gift of sight man can build upon. If fatherhood is a known adherence in your lifestyle, you adhere to the gain of being dependent on the knowledge you were taught by your parent or parents. Many find hope when they lean into the truth of the Word of God. All notable favor is righteous and good when the application of light is the component of guidance.

The author of the Word is all-knowing, and in Him is the guidance of the Most High. The gain of man is a plan of integral strength where hope resides and flourishes with unity. God brings to the table a plan and a guidance measure not otherwise found by the witness of man. Look at how God operated in the way of Ruth to Naomi. Ruth pursued the same way of being as the woman who offered her instruction of good intent. The Father of man is righteous and holy, and He is always the God of integrity. By the lead of the Savior, man is made righteous, but he must pursue the Lord in faith. God is all-knowing, so saying you trust him must be of the heart, not a simple profession of no meat. Our tie to the Lord is what determines our way ahead, and we advance in the way of tithe when our heart ignites in favor of God. Talking about Jesus is not what makes the bond formal. Our heart must unite to His person. There must be an adhering presence of God, or the unity is not maintained. The Father of mankind is a minister of great strength and bond adherence. Our God is ever faithful, and He pursues us with full garnering in the way of purpose and wise counsel. Following His way of being is the gain we all achieve when application of light is received and claimed. God does not adhere to our spirit if we reject the Son of His being. They are tied as one and cannot be separated. The grace of the King is to lead us with care, and the unity of our centered personage is righteous. Look at whom you serve. Are you secure with the guidance of light? Do you inflict harm to another, or are you responsive to the King and call on Him when in doubt?

The shoulder of Christ is available for any tears you may have falling. He will always hear your complaint. By adhering to the Lord, you invite His person to connect with you personally, where both hope and joy are filled upon you. The tithe of the heart is to embrace the mighty Word of the Lord and to apply the heart and mind in its direction. Each stanza of the Scriptures is solid in the way of enlightenment. The beverage of unity provided is never dull or unresponsive. When God connects with our person, He does so to bring a bond of love and growth to us economically in the manner of favor and support. How a person receives the Word is determined by their own tie to the Lord. If you value a righteous presence within you, your outlook will be of integral unity where you adhere to the righteous employment of God. God ties our minds to the knowledge He is the Waymaker, and in this knowledge is the path of growth desired by man to be fulfilled in the way of light. God never leaves man to decipher the knowledge of who He is without granting him the goal of understudy. He will impress upon the spirit the way to walk, and a unity will adhere if the heart is willing to gain this bond. A favor of light will be recognized, and the will of the individual will desire more of God and His presence. Rejection simply is a statement of unbelief. The faith of anyone who commits to God will adhere, and the bond will strengthen in a secure manner.

Knowing the King of man is the greatest unity available to all of mankind. There is no other bond that adheres or grows for all eternity. Your future life should reflect the care of God for you personally. A man who walks and supports the goal of God to himself is built up in the way of good intent. A strife may happen, but this is not the norm for an individual who pursues the love of the Most High. Walking in the light of God is favorable to most people even though they may not realize they walk with Christ by way of light-giving influence. But know a person is not smitten in favor of God until a complete surrender has transpired. Holding back on a gain will not bind God to you in a seamless unity. This is what sets apart a person of willing guidance to that of, someone who favors his own decision making. If you walk by way of enlightenment but finalize your choices by your own understanding, you have not made the commitment of surrender. God loves all of mankind. He supports him with daily counsel. A table setting is always a wise, gracious way to show faith, but without the gravy, potatoes are simply mashed without the power of the unified flavor of seasoning. This example is a way of guiding the recognition of a person who has a claim on God versus one who lets God claim him.

God is not a taskmaster. He is a builder of good and forthright goal-making. God operates so man is not without hope or available guidance. The light of Christ is a veil of good inspiration where favor is present and ties of commitment are made viable. The unity of God to man is a gift not accepted without the will of the individual. Purchase prices are many in the department store, but with the Lord, He paid the influence of death and brought it to its knees. Meaning the Savior is all-powerful, and by Him alone is man able to live eternally. The unity of God is forthright without the burden of nonnegotiable hindrances that lead man to hardship. Christ is always a witness of truth. In Him is the unity where all find favor when they bond with Him in a righteous manner. The way of God is to tie in complete unity so none parish or fall victim to a hardened presence of doubt. Needing to bind with the Lord is present within every heart. People who do not bond with the Savior have a spirit of dark guidance where they pursue their own way of being. Justifying the heart is how the lost work through their daily life goals, but this does not make for a life of prosperity within the spirit. Allowing the King freedom within your person is what will bring joy and hope to the heart. A life of good favor is what will ensue, and there will be gain in the way of good intent.

A person who walks with the unity of Christ is led with the goal of making trust where truth and love reside together. The lead of God to His children is purposeful and holy, just as life without God is bleak and perishing. God is a gain maker, and by Him, favor abounds. Boaz understood the Lord was righteous, and he operated in the same manner. He gifted women with the option of landholding, and he paved the way for Naomi to reside under his wing. This is a shadow of who the person of Jesus is. God is our guidance formation, and in Him, we have all the knowledge to build and claim life eternal. Our steps with light build growth, and hope is spread to the spirit of others. When a person reflects the love of God, a witness of trust is viable. The staple of light from Christ is a truth serum incorporating the love of God to man. When people show care and support, they reflect the love of God, as is His character representation. A mother who engages with solid goodness toward her child is an example of the Most High. He is generous and forthright with the goal of all that is good and holy.

The light of the King is managed by His spirit alone as we are a people group not able to withstand the glory of God in full measure. God is a presence of unity that our hearts and minds love and reflect upon. Someone who decides to turn from the love God has made an offer of is not known by Him. The connection is not adhering, and no bond has formed. The light of God is bright and secure, and it reflects trust in His person. Man cannot obtain unity by any other care that is more supportive or holy. When Christ died for mankind, it was for each and every child upon the earth. God's chosen few are the ones who choose to love Him and favor His righteous ways. God builds the network of His holy selection to that of a unity where man can be fulfilled spiritually. The bond and growth adherence is a graft of strength no one can tear apart. The lantern of unity is all-consuming. Meaning nothing can hinder the goal of love God purchased at the cross.

God designs man's heart to withstand the dark one and his claim to him. Satan is a liar, and he will inflict doubt if a breeding ground is made available. Look at the daughter-in-law who chose to return to her homeland and reject the life offering from Naomi. Her story ends abruptly with no adherence of unity from that point forward. Her stand was one of rejection, so God dismissed her as His child and let her claim her heritage of doubt and loss. God does not reject the faith He puts forward, but He does remove Himself when He is pushed away for another. The light of man is dim. The need for unity with Christ is righteous in the way it adheres the bond of strength in regard to the formation of trust and favor. If the light is a goal you find supportive, then you are still a recognized being to Christ. Your rejection of God has not been sealed for all time, so commit your heart to God and become a family member of the Most High. It is an eternal decision that has a price tag of faith and repentance. No other coin is needed, so don't feel as though you need to deposit an investment in any other form. God holds the warehouse of all wealth. What matters to Him is a personal commitment of where you tie to Him spiritually, and you believe in Him by way of His Son, the great I Am. The two act as one in the saving power of care. Investing in the good of them is a gain none can compare with. Take time to commit your heart once more and stand in the saving power of a righteous manner. Salvation is a one-time gift, but renewing your decision gifts merit to the support you have for God. Timetables change and reflect truth or a negative investment where man is either for the Lord or against Him. Unity with God brings recognition to a lifestyle of strength. Build the bond to Christ and be a saving influence for all who cross your path in trust. Your reflective way will adhere, and others will find solitude within your person.

God is not a reckoning where faith is made available upon the tired back of a nonexistent form. Faith is always on the platter of the heart of anyone who prays and reads the Bible. This promise is one of truth. God's Word never fails. It gifts unity, and God is total and complete. The enemy has no foothold over the person who is faithful in reading and adhering to the truth God has underscored since the beginning of time. The trust of God is a forthright adherence, and no one can destroy this phenomenon. Only God is a mainstay where doubt is never seen. He builds with care, and in Him is guidance and secure formations. The light of God is always a way ahead. The bounty of God to man is never something in need of growth as God is complete. However, with the intent of goodwill comes the needed form of God to man, where the desire and the aptitude of favor is realized. God's light is a signature of unity, and it adheres to the heart of man in the manner of life eternal. All God represents is truth. There is no better way of gaining trust and favor than that of pursuing the righteous Jesus. Jesus is the plan of unity, so man is able to come to the God of all there is to know. The righteous manner and intent of a person who adheres to the Lord speaks to His name and justifies the call that was given to him.

If favor has found a home in your heart, remember the crucifixion of Christ was for unity to be available, not for fame or glory. God builds in people a respect, and in this portrayal, man is able to tie his claim to the justified I Am. Without the bond of glue, the Lord maintains, no person would adhere to God in favor of Him. The bond of righteousness is a foundation where God is glorified and man is not. This is the measure of a true witness. God operates where His name is what has meaning because He is the righteous one. He is not simple or restrained in the way of bondage, but He is a standard for man to follow. Tying your heart to Christ is a wise representation, and adherence is what makes it unique. Our name is not one of recognized glory, for we are small in comparison to Christ. He alone is capable of gain in the manner of humility and outspoken care tied in trust.

God is the sight of knowledge, and He is the operative of good moral conduct. By the manner of a united bond, man, too, can dine on the luxury of righteous manner. Christ is the mechanism where hearts are glued in faith with the desire to follow the living I Am. Unity is not slight, but it is a statement of favor. All of mankind stands before God on judgment day. Whether man has given his heart to Jesus is what determines where he will reside for all time.

The Lord is a magnet, and He aligns with his true vision, offering guidance to anyone willing to prosper and grow. Building with the knowledge God is a mainstay supports the love God holds for every individual on the earth. Animals are tied to God in that He is the great Creator. He makes life exist. The future of the planet is in His hands alone. Knowing God brings favor and unity to aid the brokenhearted. Naomi was such a person, and God raised up a kinsman to offer her solitude, where she was supported and cared for in a loving manner. God abides with goodness, so look to His instruction to adhere to Him with support.

Our love is made righteous when Christ is our goal and support beam. Unity is a tie around the neck of grace which aligns with the will of the Father. Our care structure is a guarantee of gain when we lean into the call from the Lord.

God has a skill set that no other is able to accomplish. He maintains the bond of instruction where man and He are tied for all time when a heart is mindful of Him. Leaning on the wise counsel of the Bible is what makes right thinking come into view. The will of the Father is organized and structured. If you find favor has gifted you with a goal of great options, wait for the light of good unity to spring into sight. The goal of man to God is to wait and let the driving be from the backseat. God offers a path where unity is a guidance, where understanding is present, and the goal is viable. Naomi and Ruth understood the will of God was for them to return to the homeland of Naomi, thus assuring a family unit would be stable and righteous. God gives light to dreams and goals, and He makes viable the way ahead. The unity will reside, and care will be apparent. If a goal is not being met, trust the Lord has available the bond of light you need to continue to grow and prosper in unity with Him. Leaning in His direction prospers the mind and supports Him as your guidance counselor. The great I Am is not shy, nor does He fall away when the time is not at hand. He stands next to your heart, and He breathes life into your motives. If favor is forthright, there will be unity in your spirit, and you will adhere to the right purposes God has for your future. Building for the sake of making something viable is not the way of true character-making. The light of God to man is an acknowledgment that God the Father is a crafter of unity where hopes and goals align. God will grant favor to a person in need when the right motive is made representative to His person. Many factors may be hidden and out of your perspective, so grant the will of God to your person and stand in the wait. Naomi knew waiting on God's directive for her goal was to show companionship to Ruth and lead her to her home from prior days. The will of God presented a kinsman who made a recognized adhesion to the will of the Father. The timetable is not specified; however, the unity was present and made a statement of good intent by way of the offering of Ruth to Boaz. Both parties benefited and found favor. This is the bond of the Father to His people. This is what adhesion looks like. God supported the women, and He led them to support one another in care, and a direct bond of fruit became viable.

Jesus is always a way forward. Look to Christ for the goal of a lifetime. In Him, all may find rest. Naomi and Ruth found a home and a future because God was willing to serve their needs. He did not miss when he planted favor to their hearts and aligned their intent with righteous acts. Pursuing the Lord makes plain the bond and the goal of your spirit. Following in the manner of justified gain is reflective and stands with unity and forthright goals that adhere to the person of righteous trust. Belief alone is not what gains the spirit to God. One must decide to pursue the King and to make a claim to His person as their Lord in order for the root to grow and build in the way of good witness presentation. God makes it viable by way of the cross, and this is what sets in motion the bond of strength. Decide to join to Christ and you will move in a forward position where your heart will claim the great I Am and you will know Him in a personal manner with genuine love and affection.

God favors the willing with care and a manner of good bondage. The light of God is a gain and a support beam where many find advantageous grooming takes shape. If you enjoy the Word of the Lord and you desire to know each piece of Scripture, you are a witness with character. The glue has set, and you are in a place of truth. If you fail to achieve unity, even for a moment, you will notice a loss, and the Word will call to you to invest in it again. Daily is the cross one should carry by means of employing the bond and light to the spirit. God opens the mind, and He delivers the truth in a manner of faith by way of prayer and unity. How this all comes into play is by God's hand alone, not that of any individual other than Christ Jesus. The unity guidance is made clear, and understanding is measured and secure because it is always solid in Christ's presentation. The Word of God brings truth and light. There is never a Scripture verse that is a false lead, so when you apply the structure of growth, a witness takes form and lives within you. God operates with clear intent, so you won't feel misguided or misled. In Him is the unique ability to speak to every person in relation to their own understanding. God is light, and in Him is truth. There is no fault of misguided influence, so you are safe in His care. Desiring to adhere to the King is a wise choice. Favor is seen as sure-footed, so invest in the righteous manner of God and find favor that supports your every move. Living for Jesus is wise and trustworthy. Align your goal-making with the great I Am and know a resolve of peace and security in a righteous way of being.

God clarifies the bond of righteous behavior. His glue cements the mind, and it bonds with His person. The Father is righteous and good at all times. Many find faith a support beam, and they adhere to the underlined Word of truth. In doing so, recognizing when the enemy strikes becomes more prevalent. The power of God is wholesome and righteous. It does not have a price tag of friendship where the heart is led to a draw of doubt or an adhering manner of disrespect. The lead of God to man does not harbor an ulterior agenda, nor will it represent in a claim of unity where man is not righteous. God is respectful to the people He adores. His will is ever-abundant and made clear. Should an avenue of influence enter your center thought process, determine what the light resembles. If you are enticed by the pull of favor, but it is not in alignment with true worship of the King, you are being misled, and an assault is staking against your person. Recognizing this affront may come with an intense need for communicating and bonding. A red flag will alert your heart, and you will know mischief is at work. When unity is on the table, an influence of desire will not be out of the will of the Father. A gain of inheritance will be made viable, and you will lean into the Savior with wise assertations. God is light and promise where you underline good intent. The wise action of resistance is what stakes a claim toward the unity of God to your spirit. A goal of appreciation can be interpreted as an advance and lead in the direction of loss. Stay focused on the knowledge you require, the safety net of Christ to be able to walk in care and upright unity. He will guide you when temptation is on the scene, and He will make a stand where you resist the pull it has, and you walk away. Listening to the Lord is what will bind your spirit to Him and keep your thought process precise and stable.

Unity is an element that is planned in a manner of trust by God to His people. His enlightened heart adjusts to the goal of a tied mainframe where God to man is a binding of strength. God is the one with the gain unit, and He applies His knowledge to man by way of the saving power of Jesus. The blood of Christ is solid and holy. It purifies and cleanses the witness of man when acceptance and care have been made viable. God's power is the manner of binding goal setting, and in Him is the light of growth. God illuminates the heart, and He declares His love to man by way of spiritual unity supporting love and care. Trust is what adheres to the unity, and it engages the thought process to grow and care for others just as Christ cares for all. Our knowledge of the Lord is minimal yet righteous. The favor of God to our person is enlightenment and wise support. Knowing the Lord is called by man to be saved from sin brings the light of knowledge in the Master Himself.

Christ the Lord is a cultivator of good intent, and in Him is a righteous love, caring, and lit in truth. All of our understanding is not viable until we incline our support toward the unity God offers. Jesus is the Waymaker, and He is our standard for strength. In God, we find favor and light. The unity is made viable when we trust and adhere to the will of the Father. If a bounty comes within reach, yet it holds a temptation outside of the love God holds for man, resist it and forget the temptation. Remove yourself from the possible attraction and stand in the safety zone of freedom. Satan has many accomplished skill tactics. He knows what your enticing features are, and he has influence over your mind, but know he cannot operate where he is not welcome. If the door closes and no footwear is in sight, he will rescind his plan and not adhere to you in the manner of spiritual control. He has no power if light is present and the bond of God to a heart stands against him.

The character of the man called freedom is Christ Jesus. He is ever available to build a relationship with. Lean into Him and have unity by way of His shield to your person. God operates in the know, and He supports the love you own as a goal in unity. When the Lord is the caretaker of your spirit, you adhere to Him in a personal manner, and gain comes forth. The unity of God with your kindred heart is ever precious and holy. The unity of the King is set in stone, so nothing can tear apart the love God has for each person on earth. Knowing whom you serve is what awakens the thought process and leads it in response to the call of Christ.

Tails of the kangaroo are sturdy, and they support the body framework when they are being assaulted. But the strength is not tied to the will of the Father as a unity of faith. The example above is merely the accepted unity of physical bonding. God designed the kangaroo to glide in the way of hopping, yet it doesn't tip over or fall forward. The legs support the back, and a balance is made viable. Each animal on earth has been designed by the hand of God. There are no mistakes, and the unity is pure. God offers man the gain of being head of all creatures. This position is not to be taken loosely or with an assault intent.

Lending in the way of care for animals is a tie of goodness that builds the bond of good form. A lead of good influence is what sets in motion the Father and His manner of light. God builds in favor of support of wise accordance and truth as a barrier for the mind and heart. Love is not an influence of darkness. A liable path will contain the unity of God the Father, and His presence will decorate the lead. God applies a measure man cannot adhere to without the proactive front of faith and a connection in the way of guidance. Meaning that God's beauty is understood without a dark inhibitor as the mainstay. In the event you are under deceptive encounters, look at the manner in which the formula came into being. Were you unaware of a destructive gain in force, and the level of doubt had crossed your spirit? Recognizing the dark form will be a witness to your spirit, and you will know if the plant is righteous or one of dark depravity. Allow the will of the Father to be your subconscious and make your stand a solid unity with Christ. If you stumble and fall, remove the temptation and stand in a solid way of presentation. Adulteress maneuvers happen when an individual fancies a life outside of the marriage bed, which in actuality is a mere trap to sever the love of God from the heart. Leaning into another individual in place of your partner is an example of loss, not gain. You are deceived and on the path of unity with the dark one. The deceptive way the enemy leads you will rise up in the form of temptation, where the heart and mind fall in line with the goal of the flesh. Stimulation of the body is a powerful pull, but know it is not of God. When the insight of the skin reflects in alarm, recognize the intent and leave the situation in the dust. Set a standard of trust and guide your heart and mind to clarity by reading the Word of God. It will support you, and you will find strength where you will adhere to the love of the Father, and no tantalizing suggestive offer will adhere to your person. You will stand in complete control and walk in a steadfast gate. Take a look at the support of God in the way of Naomi when she felt weak and abandoned. She returned home to safe measures where her family resided and lived under the protection of Christ's wing. The tantalization of gain came with the Lord and the supply method He made available where strength and understanding ensued. God's love awakens the bond of great unity, and a plan of solid measure will adhere. The light will be viable, and unity will carve out a stand in the way of instruction. The heart will know the adhesive glue, and it will be led in truth. The stand of the neck is what situates the heart, so think on the righteous way of living, and you will gain in the way of true moral insight. God gifts the light, and through His person, we are made whole. Our manner of gifts will not lead to debauchery but to that of good intent and solid justification. God offers a reprieve for the heart, and then the physical need blends away in a calm retreat.

Robin) (Rochel) Arne

Unity Maker Six

God Supports All of Mankind

God loves all of mankind, and He never loses the connection one makes to Him.

The love God offers is a path of justified hope where all of God is faithful and good. Build in favor of trust and know the Lord operates in unity with your spirit. A plan of good intent supports the goal of righteous will, and God is at the helm when this is transpiring. Lean into the Father and know Him in a personal manner. The gift of the Bible will pose as the measure where you glue to the King and support Him with your heart. The favor of God is ever before man. God builds in the unit of heart to mind. This means that all of the focus we apply toward the study of the Word will aid our mind in its deciphering of what to align with. Satan attacks when we let in a dark hope. Stand in the goal of light and lean into the will of God by reading the Bible and knowing the will of the Father. In the act of bondship, you will adhere and have a bounty of strength, and the knowledge of the heart will supersede the mind's attraction to false impressions. When alignment begins to form, enact the pole of truth and recognize your intent. If good is what the forecast presents, with no sin factor or loss to others, you have a righteous goal before you. However, man will lie to himself and make a claim to support his need for the flesh to feel gratified.

Look to the Word of the Lord to determine the truth of your goal. Has a deceptive guardian laid claim to your wisdom, or have you turned toward the pursuit of strength? If you follow in the way of good intent, your spirit will align, and you will recognize a false impression has no standing within you. God leads with the glue of positive gain. When a heart desires a return outside of favor from on high, Satan is manifesting as a source of false light. In doing so, the available way of tying the heart to the center of understanding will be made light if God is the one you turn to. Know God does not abandon His people no matter the claim against Him. Follow the goal where support and trust are bound as a unit of opportunity. If a fellow believer has lost the path of unity and you see the sin projected, speak to him with confidence and guide him into the light once again. Honest goal recognition is what maintains the heart and mind with Christ, so evaluate your dream and make it justified. The will of God will mold your hope, and a plan of purpose will unfold. In the event you have grown a false manifestation, wait for God to rectify the intent into one of good moral unity. A clear bond of growth will adhere, and you will be a witness to the light in the manner of a build that supports the love of God to His people in the way of opportunity and care. God is the viable truth and the hope of good intent. Without the love of the Most High, there is no real opportunity that lasts through all of time. In favor of support is the body of faith. When the bond of truth is viable, unity is a bright stand, and hope is recognized. When a person has a goal but no truth in the making, a false desire will arise. There will be no viable way to obtain the desire, and you will end in defeat. Know the Lord works in His timing, so build with the support of His person. When your purpose is right and true, you will lean into the fold of love the Father presents, and the unity of just cause will be viable. God does not favor one person before another, but He does make options in the form of trust. Know the Lord plants a dream when the heart aligns with His person. If you have been in alignment and no available path has been presented, stand in the gap and trust the Lord is going to act on your behalf. Testing does come into play, so wait upon the unity to present as a whole. God knows the true character of any man. He will organize a dream and make it portray as justified and the length of desire may not be a slight goal of stand. Unity is the purpose of God to man not the build itself. Trust is what sets in motion the love of God to your heart. If you favor your goal above the love of the Father, the wait may be one of growth where you are bonding to the Lord with support in the way of recognized harmony leading to unity. Testing is not a trial but a proofing system where you bond to the Father in a more personal manner. Think about the travel time era when horse and buggy or mule and cart were the mode of transportation. Man needed to align with the structure of the whole provision for the road, or a loss would ensue. Just as man needs the knowledge of provision for a vacation stay, he also needs the guidance of God to obtain a bond of length that supports all time.

The light of the Father is made viable when man ties in unity by way of prayer and reading of the Word. If you adjust your lifestyle to that of true commitment, your source of truth will be the Word of God. You will adhere to the knowledge God is the great I Am and He is always justified and pure. Learning the truth depends on the willing heart of man. Not all people lean into the Word and believe completely. Some determine the laws of God are too restrictive, and they lose the desire to follow Him in the way of unity and trust. Abandoning the love of God is an eternal loss that can't be retrieved if the heart has committed to the dark one. There is no in-between. The two manifestations are light and dark. God is the light within us, and Satan is the dark ruler for a time. One day he will lose all attempts to destroy as God is going to seal his fate in the lake of fire. He will have no hope of ever leading another person to hell. Invest in the wise presence of Christ and pursue Him in the manner of faith. By your witness, you will be judged, and your profession today is what cements your life eternal. Look at the offering of Naomi to the righteous life for Ruth. She delivered the unity and granted the good God had given her by way of a husband and son who supported the great I Am. The family tie was solid, and the truth of God was in them. Ruth favored the life Naomi reflected, and she bonded in character to her person. In the same manner, God grafts to our hearts who He is and how He builds our goals and studies of life. Knowing the Lord is favor and guidance where truth resides. God brings clarity and guidance when we subject our hearts and minds to Him in a personal manner. The gift of instruction is suggestive, where truth is the bond that claims our offering of trust. God is ever faithful. In Him is support and light of good intent. Know the Lord and have a seal of strength on your heart. In doing so, you will adhere in the way of secure moral justification leading to growth and a witness of love.

God builds and guards the heart. He never destroys a goal if it is justified and clear with support from on high. The leverage of God to man is unique, where there is unity and forthright bonding. If you desire a life outside of Jesus, know you have chosen to walk in the way of loss, not gain. Only with God is there favor and support. Only by His lead is there strength and hope for a life of good intent with moral righteousness abounding. The love of God is always good and true. You never have to doubt the Father will lead in a stiff manner. He is gentle and kind, and through His knowledge, you will thrive and bloom. Loving God is fruitful and wise, so take the opportunity before you and build in the way of great things, as this is the way of God. A build of light is a gift of support. The Father has a goal of strength and unity, so knowing Him in a personal way is the guidance measure of true righteous gifting.

The center of your thinking needs to be that of God and Him alone. If your dream is so grand in your spirit that it consumes your thought process, it has become your God. Align with the Father and pray for truth. He will make a viable acceptance to the goal where you place it on the shelf for there to be adhesion to the King. Once you have obtained the bond of God to your spirit where God the Father consumes your goal, know the King is planted securely within your heart. If building is all you insist upon, that too may be a hindrance to your growth. Lean into the love God offers and dine on the solitude of God Himself. Let His way of being be your focus. Know the love of the Father above that of all else, then you will be justified and respectful to the will of God and His plan for you. Timing is always what sets man alive with intent. Wait on God to reveal His light so you adhere to Him in the righteous tone He supports. If unity is made viable, you will adhere to the prospect of waiting, and the truth of your support guidance will come into the arena of your heart. Work is important, but it must not be your focus above all else. Reading God's Word will align your thought process, and you will desire the true way of being God puts forth.

The struggle for man is his willingness to create without the will of God. Man desires to grow and blossom where he has designed a prosperous unity with himself. Bonding in the form of hope does not adhere to the will of God simply because it reflects labor. Boaz built-in landownership when he determined to accept Ruth as his wife, but he did not pursue her for the wealth. His goal was to provide for her and Naomi and be recognized as a kinsman redeemer who had God as his support beam. If bonding to another attraction is all-consuming, let your actions reflect the love God holds for all by stepping back and practicing unity with Christ. This comes by way of reading the Word of God and applying it toward the heart by way of reflective counsel. If light is your intent and you desire more of God and not less, you are growing in favor of truth. Your understanding is genuine, and your goals are aligned with the Savior.

Growing in favor supports the will of the Father, and in Him is guidance and pure motives. Look at where man has placed his goal-making in the way of support to know who he claims as Lord. People reflect their support beam, and they invite the knowledge toward their hearts even if they haven't professed allegiance. It is viable as there is but one God. Anything outside of Him is not genuine. It is darkness. The force of good is a plant of light. It stands the test of time, and it won't fade or wash away on judgment day. Christ the Lord is a morally wholesome being. In Him alone is the insight of truth and support. The lead of God is righteous and holy. The God of all mankind supports the favor of justified manners. His goal is to align with the will of the Father and be united in care. Offering to another the learned manner of good intent sets one in favor with God. If you package material and do it in a holy, gifted, wise way, you are honoring the will of the Lord. Even daycare supports the will of the Father. It is the fruit of the vine, and it connects with Him as a whole. The body of faith is tied to the lead of man if it doesn't adhere to the will of God. There can be belief without true spiritual guidance in the way of truth. God does not operate on a slant. In Him is the light of hope and strength. God sets in motion an aligned manner, and good form arises. The value of man to God is limited where man's abilities are few. God is all-knowing, and He is able to abide in favor always. God builds the landmark of solid, righteous gifts. Tying a person to a chair is an example of something evil working. God acts righteously, yet He claims man to Himself, and He organizes the heart and mind to conquer the dark element. Only God is righteous, and through His character, we are made right. The power of wise counsel is at the helm of the heart when Scripture is applied and studied. Knowing the will of God is a gift and unity of insight. Allow the body of faith to entail your spirit and connect in the way of favor from on high. The favor of God to man is unity and support. The leadership of God is righteous and pure, whereas man fails at goal-making. Man desires to build, but it is by the witness of Christ that man abides with unity. The light of God is ever before our hearts. He performs the unity by way of spiritual adherence and support. So, understand you need the Lord's presence to achieve upright goals and bonds of light. The promise of the King is a tie of strength that no other can claim. The cross is a signature memory dispersed across the globe, and it will never dissipate. No one can remove the truth, as God is the giver of the knowledge it presents.

A measure of support is valid if God orchestrated the motion. Take a look at how man forms a unity. It is shallow and void of true gain. Marriages fail often, and bountiful aspects are lost. Man does not adhere in the way of genuine good enlightenment. The favor of God is all good and holy. Through the love of God, man compiles a to-do thought process, but the recognition of light is made viable when trust enters goal-making. God allows man to recreate His objective, but know God is the great I Am.

There is nothing man has developed that God didn't manufacture for him in talent or understanding. A light shines brightest when the favor of hope has been planted and adhered to. Knowing the will of God is a bounty and a desire for all of mankind. Man may not realize his call, but the truth is written upon the heart. God leads all of mankind. He is a permanent part of our makeup. We lean into the love of God, and we support the knowledge God is who He claims to be. The way of gain supports the God of all. The value you place on the recognition of truth is what maintains the unity and makes it complete. If facts are something you respond to, research the manner of the building of Boaz in the decision to become a kinsman redeemer. He was not the first in line to garner gain by way of Ruth's property as it required another to step forward and claim the growth. This requirement maintained the boundary line and built upon it, but when the transaction was complete, the property would then rest in the hands of the rightful owner. That person would have been seen as righteous in the way of unity. A female was not permitted to gain income from farm grounds. Males were the entitled signatures placed upon the receipt of sale. However, in the event of children, the property would transfer to them, making the lineage stand as rightful heirs.

God has a purpose for the women of today, just as He did in the early times of the written Scriptures. The call for a woman of this day may even include ministry in a body of faith. Women are considered fair in their manner but not ignorant. Many men are not supportive of the growth and recognition, but the influence of the female persuasion is coherent when the application of the written Word is applied. The faith presented is what sets apart a true witness. In the day of Ruth, women were not permitted to hold a title, but that is no longer the case. That is where the management of goods and services now reside. Land ownership is also available to the female body of faith. A church is now a home to the woman. In prior days, men had to share what transpired in a fellowship gathering of faith support. God has grown favor toward the female, and He has given her support.

All titles now reflect ownership by way of payment, and lineage is not what determines the value of assets. God has developed for man an incentive where work and ambition maintain the unity of care for income and support. God permits all to acquire gain in some form of value of heart to Christ. Meaning we are the goal-setters. How we apply our hearts and minds is what sets in motion the tie and strength of unity. The developer of good intent is our own understanding and our own desire. If we enjoy providing care and structure to one another, our heart is aligned with the Lord. Jesus died for our sins, and He offered His heart to all of mankind without a price or will of goods to retain the gift. We are freely given, and so we ourselves should freely give in return. A ministry is made of people with the goal of sharing whom they know and trust. God is the unity maker and the provider. By the revelation of God to man, there is a knowledge that God is all-powerful. The reflective support we align our hearts to stands as the witness we will claim on judgment day. The offering will have a root, or it will not be present. How man has built in the way of following the will of God will be viable and made plain. God crafts the heart along with the goal of bonding with His person. Man is able to stand apart from God if he so chooses, but then the curtain of strength will not adhere. If the value is placed on the gift and received as truth, a bond and light will enter the mind, and the truth will glue the Scripture of unity to the will of the individual. The truth will adhere, and bounty will thrive.

The unity of Christ is a goal of trust where the heart experiences the light and builds in its recognized glow. God is all-knowing, and He designed the heart and mind, so He is capable of understanding the operations of them both. Nothing is hidden from the Lord. He knows every detail and thought process. Your darkest times are recorded and washed by blood if you follow and pursue the Lord as Savior. Understanding the Lord is righteous gifts us with the knowledge He operates for our favor. We are not small in His eyes. He adores us with care and He desires for us to thrive. He works in unity, and He adjusts the light to shine in our favor. The righteous way He builds our hearts and minds is a glorious presentation of trust between Him and ourselves. God is a peacekeeper. He is made of truth, and He alone crafts all that is right. In knowing the Lord, you adjust your thinking, and you gain by way of intellect. The light of the King is vibrant and clear. He does not cast a shadow of dark oppression. The value of The King is good, and He is trustworthy. By a witness of knowledge, one is made viable in the way of unity. When you favor God, you esteem the goal of relational hope and leadership. God is a goalkeeper. He organizes the mind and secures it in a righteous manner. He evaluates the heart and leads it to righteous atonement in the way of truth and a garnered adherence in trust. The timetable of faith is justified and holy. The person of Jesus is righteous above all others. None can support man in the manner of God. He is superior and a unity maker of light. God is the one to operate in faith and build our hearts and minds with glue of gain. The light of God is where trust and hope abide and are tied to the spirit with mutual appreciation. Knowing the Lord is what determines the eternal bond and where one resides upon death.

God is the being where man is supported with all good intent. God aligns the will of those who pursue Him in trust and support by way of a unified goal of mutual bonding. When faith is built upon, much favor is bestowed on the heart of the willing person of trust and unity. God crafts in alignment of true ownership by way of the saving power of the Lord. Upon the witness of confession, Jesus procures the heart and claims it for the Father. The two act as one, and a cleaning ensues where the heart is washed clean with repentance and support of the great I Am. Our own study of the Word determines how close we become to the Lord and how our favor toward Him unites. The goal of God is for our spirit to align with His and meet with a unified guest of love and structure. The unity is a graft of intellect and the united bond flourishes with support. We tie with care, and we become holy in the way of gifted knowledge where we operate with justified actions supporting the love of God, and His way of being becomes our unity.

God is our reflective desire when we adhere to His person. That is why we need His growth within our person. We are not able to adhere to Him unless we apply our hearts and minds toward Him in unity. Reading the Word of God builds the bond and makes it right with strength and support. The Bible is a book of love. It stands as the way of guidance in knowing the favor of God. Through the representation it ascribes to, clarity is made viable. The gift it casts is knowledge, and a path of righteous goals are built upon.

When a plan is in formation, building requires the heart to inject the goal of strength, where unity is needed to align with Christ. Knowing the Lord will aid the building technique and square the goal into righteous maneuvers, leading to a plan of forthright gain. The Great I Am offers the guidance and the needed plan building to entertain in wise decision-making when applying knowledge to goal setting. A pathway will arise, and you will have a witness of integrity aligned with the Father, and His way of being will be visible. Trust is the magnet of strength, building character and guidance in faith and unity. Giving God the freedom to bind us to Him for the better of our own gain is not something to take lightly. It is a stable unity where our hearts and minds correlate and support the love God holds for us, and we lean into the good He makes available. The unity of God to man is ever forthright and justified. The person of God is a wholesome being. He is a mainframe of care and support where all we need is made viable. Even death cannot overcome our hearts and minds, as Jesus overcame death on the cross. The resurrection stands for all time. It is never going to fade or lose footing. The manner of the light the King presents is always going to shine. God is a planter of good intent. Lean into the knowledge He is ever at our call. The unity in prayer is right and true. The flavor of God is wholesome and justified by way of pure processes and guidance.

Christ can be adhered to through the witness of prayer. Bending to the will of the Father is to know Him in a personal manner. This happens when the love you hold speaks to the knowledge, and you claim a righteous plant with the Savior. Prayer supports the bond, and knowledge plants trust. Work toward the understanding of Naomi when she shared her trust with Ruth by way of leading them both toward a home base where the family resided. The Father supports our unity with fellow companions, and He desires for us to stay connected to the people around us in the manner of visiting and regular support contact. Knowing the Father guards our hearts and we visualize His good practices as our own. A leader of wise understanding leads with support and, in doing so, adheres to the will of the Father. If you have talked to many concerning God, you have stood as a proclamation to the witness that God is the great I Am. The level of instruction is not what determines the bond of man with God. It is the intent and the justified way of presenting the knowledge you contain. Any person who speaks freely about the risen Lord is declaring His faith and procuring a righteous foothold in the way of unity for an eternal witness upon judgment day. No one's influence is above another's. Each bounty of favor comes from God's support, so know you witness in faith and guidance from God. Teaching the Word is a gift, and those who offer the hand of light have a basket of favor upon their hearts and minds. Guiding someone to the Lord is not of little consequence.

The knowledge of unity is right and justified, and it is solid and holy when the will of the Father is the goal. The Bible teaches the Word, and by the will of God, much favor is bestowed to the weary. Knowing God is forthright, and it binds the love of anyone who worships the King, and it leads them to a solid foundation of good gain. The righteous manner of living is a beacon of truth when the applied field of unity is with the Savior and not his counterpart. Satan is not a being of light. He is not capable of leading anyone into care or support. Even the dark light he gifts is false. When the pocketbook fills due to false, inherit witnessing no true moral, uplifting favor is bestowed. Only loss will ensue, and there will reside more darkness. You need to lean into the Father for clear support; otherwise, all you know will be for naught. Trust is the binding factor where man can accept the offering of salvation. Look to how Naomi guided Ruth in care and knowledge of who her people regarded as justified. Knowing the great I Am is what determines the bond of light or favor. The King is supportive and wise in His presentation to the spirit. He does not offer a bond of negative hope. Salvation is a goal of aligned strength and support. The power of God is wholesome and pure, so knowing the acceptance of His person grants unity and a way of dignified favor.

About the Author

Robin has the goal of sharing the unity of the one who claims victory for her at the cross. Jesus is the mainstay and the character of her heart. God is the great Word of truth. Sharing His person is the desire she presents at every turn of the heart. The knowledge of God is written within her person, and she offers her gain to many. Writing presents the available doorway for her to communicate on a regular basis. Her flagship day is one of sharing the Biblical truth in a constructive manner of good intent. Many have found favor by following her on the web, Facebook, MeWe, and Twitter. Her account is made public so anyone with the desire to hear her thoughts is able to glean her refreshing words of optimism. The insight she holds is a witness to her adherence to the Bible. Robin instructs through the process of maintenance and has a willing drive to share the Scriptures. She freely gives her knowledge, and she offers others care by way of administering goals of value. The dining of the fruit comes by way of notable adhering to the Word and the support value it holds. Christ is the reason Robin authors material for others to gain from. She enjoys the process of writing, and her set, moral path folds like a chapter of precise, wise structure due to the author of the Bible, God Himself. The thought process is made viable as the knowledge is spirit gained. Today is a time of good form, so read with care and know the Lord through the eyes of truth by way of support and adherence to the Word. Just as this book expresses the unity of Ruth, Robin's other works of written structure portray truth to that of financial wisdom in knowing the care of God. Trust the message of unity and lean into the Gospel as a whole.

Robin Arne is available for author interviews. For more information contact us at info@advbooks.com

To purchase additional copies of these books, visit our bookstore at
www.advbookstore.com

*A*dvantage
BOOKS

"we bring dreams to life"™
www.advbookstore.com